A Conservative Consensus?

Housing policy before 1997 and after

Peter King

imprint-academic.com

Copyright © Peter King, 2006

The moral rights of the author have been asserted.
No part of any contribution may be reproduced in any form
without permission, except for the quotation of brief passages
in criticism and discussion.

Published in the UK by
Imprint Academic, PO Box 200, Exeter EX5 5YX, UK

Published in the USA by
Imprint Academic, Philosophy Documentation Center
PO Box 7147, Charlottesville, VA 22906-7147, USA

ISBN-10 1 84540 046 1
ISBN-13 9781845400460

A CIP catalogue record for this book is available from the
British Library and US Library of Congress

Contents

Preface	1
Introduction: Ideas and Housing	5
1 Conservatism	21
2 The Influence of Libertarianism	47
3 Ideology or Pragmatism?	65
4 Conservative Housing Policy	73
5 Housing Policy after 1997	99
6 But is it Conservative?	121
Conclusion: Keeping Things Close	141
Bibliography	149
Index	154

To those closest to me:

B, H and R

Preface

One of the things that has both amused and frustrated me over the last few years is the near desperation of the left to hold on to their certainties.

The amusement derives from seeing something of a nervous collapse going on within many on the left. They despised everything to do with Thatcher and the Conservatives during the 1980s and 1990s and doubtless many worked hard to achieve the eventual demise of the right in 1997. However, instead of seeing the end of Conservative ideas and the start of a new golden age of socialist transformation, many on the left have had to sit on their hands whilst New Labour has promoted choice, talked tough on asylum and immigration, and even gone to war in support of a right-wing American president. Most telling of all is the phrase that seems to be used at the end of every conversation about Blair and New Labour: 'At least it's not the Tories'.

The frustration comes from reflecting on this desperate attempt at justification. To all intents and purposes it might as well be the Tories, because the only difference is that the tribe that is currently in charge doing Tory things calls itself the Labour party. It is as if saying 'At least it's not the Tories' makes this reality go away. But of course, it will not simply go away, and what is frustrating is the inability of the left to come to terms with how things have changed. In particular there is a refusal to understand the significance of a supposed centre-left party ruling as if it were conservative. Of course, many on the left have their answers ready, most of which can be based around the apparent pervasiveness of global capitalism: the Blair government is merely bending to the whims of global capital, in thrall to the evil American empire, and so on in its tiresomely predictable way. These answers have the same advantage that they have always had: they have the virtue of offering a total answer and are incapable of disproof. Indeed, even to argue against them is seen as a sure sign of global capitalism at its dire work.

This book is born out of this sense of frustration. In particular, what does it really mean just to say 'At least it's not the Tories' when we have a government that is doing pretty much what the Tories would be doing? And what if this has nothing to do with global capitalism but actually comes out of an understanding of what people want and expect from government? Of course, this might be because most people consider that on balance global capitalism is better than the available alternative — global poverty — and that it suits their lifestyle rather well. Most social scientists might deplore this, but at least they get to share the lifestyle.

So in this book I want to take seriously the conservative world view and the proposition that it might actually be linked to something other than selfishness and the interests of big business. I want to try to understand why conservative ideas are so tenacious and apparently pervasive, so that they even thrive and develop when the Conservative party has been in electoral freefall and the Labour party can win an unprecedented third term. Or, in other words, why is it that a conservative electorate can trust a centre-left party to run the country without fear of it running amok and doing anything socialist? Might it be that the conservative disposition is now so ingrained that the actual results of elections no longer matter?

It is my view that housing — or rather property — plays an important role in this, and that we need to understand how we use our housing if we are to grasp the politics of housing, and how this links with the conservative disposition. Of course, housing does not win or lose elections. However, it is my view that our housing allows us to hide away from politics and to avoid elections in the knowledge that they do not matter. Housing has a depoliticising effect on us, just as the politics have been taken out of housing by the growth of owner occupation over the last twenty five years. So I do not want to claim, as the Conservatives certainly did and Saunders (1990) appeared to do, that there is a link between owner occupation and voting Tory. Rather I want to argue something rather more fundamental: that owner occupation is a key confirmation of the conservative disposition. My view is not that we become more conservative because of owner occupation — although some might have — but that we are attracted to owner occupation because we are conservative.

The distinction between conservatism and Conservatism is important here, with only the latter denoting anything definite in terms of politics. The argument I seek to develop here is that conservatism can and should be seen as cultural rather than merely political. If we see conservatism as the *cultural condition of politics* — as the disposition that conditions our attitude towards politics — we can start to understand how we can have an apparently modernising centre-left government that is also conservative.

Some commentators on the left have begun to grasp something of this cultural disposition, particularly Giddens (1994) and his discussion of how it is the erstwhile radicals of the left, such as trade unionists and environmentalists who have found themselves having to concern themselves with preserving the status quo. According to Giddens it was the right, led by figures such as Reagan and Thatcher, who appeared radical, with the left seeming to be the reactionaries. From this he developed the idea of *philosophical conservatism*, where one is predisposed to resist change, albeit perhaps only on certain issues and for a certain period of time. As I discuss in chapter one, we should not confuse Giddens's notion with conservatism *per se* — there is more to the disposition than reacting against those things we do not like and which threaten our own interests (O'Hara, 2005). However, Giddens is correct in suggesting that we do have a predisposition to cling to what is near to us, and to see this as more significant than what is far away. This does not apply to all of us, and even when it does it may not dominate to the exclusion of all else. However, we need to recognise it and deal with its effects, especially when we appear to have politicians like Reagan, Thatcher and Blair who are all able to tap into it.

This book is sympathetic to what I have termed the conservative disposition, and this may make it unique within the housing literature. However, my aim is not to offer support to any particular political programme or party. Indeed it is my contention that we can find the conservative disposition alive and active in more than one party of the main British political parties. This book is critical of housing policy of both left and right. There is much in Conservative housing policy that I do not support, particularly the tendency to over centralise. I would also suggest that there is no little or no justification for maintaining the Right to Buy. My aim — and this is particularly clear in the discussion on the Right to Buy — is not particularly to offer support, but to show why it was successful as a policy. Likewise, I am critical of the style and language of New Labour, but can still appreciate how and why it has been so important politically, even as the language serves mainly to mask a rather unfortunate combination of timidity and cynicism. New Labour's language has resonated with a common-sense view of the self which appreciates notions such as choice, responsibility and respect. My intention in discussing both the Conservatives and New Labour is to put the policies into their proper context so that we can understand the degree of continuity there has been over the last twenty five years. Many may find this continuity regrettable, but it is hard to avoid the conclusion that it exists. Accordingly, we need to understand what the basis is for it, if only to better fight against it.

This book does connect up with some of my recent work on privacy and subjectivism, if not always in a direct way. It has been my contention in my last two books — *Private Dwelling* (2004) and *The Common Place* (2005) — that housing can only be properly understood if we see it as an essentially private activity based around notions of security, complacency (or ordinariness) and the primary locus of protected intimacy. In this new book I try to connect this sense of housing to the broader policy context. I do this most obviously, if still briefly, in the introduction and conclusion where I seek to show the importance of property to the conservative disposition and hence why politicians of both parties have sought to place property ownership as the centrepiece of their housing policies. My aim therefore is not to be controversial for its own sake, but to put across what I consider to be a serious and considered argument with far-reaching implications for the way we understand housing and how it impacts politically.

I have several people to thank for their help in the writing of this book. My colleagues at the Centre for Comparative Housing Research have continued to provide a challenging and productive environment in which to develop ideas. In particular, Tim Brown has offered comments and advice on parts of this book, and this has improved it considerably. Likewise, I am grateful to the many students who have listened and responded to some of these ideas. Their comments have helped enormously. My family has been tremendously supportive and encouraging in this book, as with my previous projects. My wife, Barbara, is a valuable and critical sounding-board for my ideas, as well as undertaking the onerous and entirely unreasonable task of proofreading the entire text. My two daughters, Helen and Rachel, have shown an increasing interest in this project as it has developed and have been patient enough to listen to my moans and worries about its progress. I therefore dedicate this book to these three wonderful people who are miraculously still disposed towards me.

Introduction
Ideas and Housing

We are all Conservatives Now

Why should we bother with conservatism[1] any more? Indeed, it might seem wilfully perverse to concentrate on such ideas in Britain after three election defeats for the Conservative party, and after nearly a decade of New Labour. The more generous might concede that conservatism is of some historical interest, and we might learn something from this. However, to talk of a conservative consensus, such that it is implied that conservatism remains relevant to the present and the future is taking things rather too far. Of course, most academics and commentators writing about housing in Britain would not see this as particularly problematical. For them the Thatcher period was an unfortunate and misguided time that sent housing policy in entirely the wrong direction. Accordingly, the housing policies that came out of it, particularly the Right to Buy and the support for owner occupation, were, at best, regrettable and at worst, disastrous.

Now there is fortunately no correlation between weight of numbers and being correct, otherwise these academics would have had to concede something very significant after four straight Conservative election victories between 1979 and 1992. Therefore, in what follows I wish to present the case that housing policy — current policy in and around the year 2006, and not just in the past — is based around a conservative consensus. This consensus was forged in the period between 1979 and 1997 but has been extended and to an extent strengthened by the policies of New Labour since 1997.

---

[1] As I explain in chapter one, I differentiate between conservatism as a series of ideas that does not relate to any particular party or set of institutions, and the Conservative party by the use of lower and upper case respectively.

This is admittedly a controversial thesis, and one that will be resisted by those who support New Labour, as well as those who see any taint of conservatism as unacceptable and in need of immediate eradication. Yet it is one that I shall hang on to tenaciously throughout this book, in the hope that by the end I might have persuaded at least some of its readers of the strength of my case.

It is my view, therefore, that if we wish to understand housing as it currently is we need to look backwards to the policies made between 1979 and 1997 (and indeed even earlier), but that then we also need to view these policies through the prism of what I shall term the *conservative disposition*. This sense of the world, which centres on pragmatism, scepticism towards government and a desire for property ownership, is what has created the current attitudes towards housing that governments over the last twenty five years have responded to.

But even if this were not the case there would still be a need to understand the 1979–97 period and the housing policies that came out of it. First, the Conservatives were in office for so long that they were able to make many structural changes and to alter the culture in which housing policy and housing organisation operated. In short, the Conservative governments under Thatcher and Major created the framework in which current policy still sits. The major housing acts in 1980, 1988 and 1989 still set the structural context, and attitudes towards the major tenures solidified as a result of these policies towards owner occupation and social housing.

Indeed, there has been nothing since 1997 to match the vision or sense of purpose of a policy such as the Right to Buy or the intellectual clarity and forthrightness of the 1987 Housing White Paper (DOE, 1987). As *Roof Briefing* (no. 39, April 2000, p. 2) commented immediately after the publication of the 2000 Housing Green Paper: 'This is a managerial rather than an ideological green paper, producing an avalanche of new procedures from every nook and cranny of the housing sector. But the big picture remains the same'. It goes on to state that the Green Paper, 'will not herald a sea change like the 1980 Act's Right to Buy or the 1988 Act's deregulation of private renting and the switch to private finance'. This was despite the fact that the Blair government announced the Green Paper as being the first comprehensive review of housing policy in twenty three years. If this really was the case then one would have to conclude that there was not much that was wrong. Indeed the one phrase that rang out of the 2000 housing Green Paper — perhaps because it was used three times — was 'Most people are well housed' (DETR/DSS, 2000, pp. 7, 15, 20). This can be read as an implicit recognition that New Labour found much to agree with in pre-1997 policies.

What this suggests, then, is that much of policy since 1997 has been about extending existing mechanisms and tinkering at the margins. Therefore if we want to understand where current policies come from, and why they have such longevity, we need to go back to before New Labour and look at the ideas of those who actually formulated and implemented them.

In any case, no government exists in a vacuum, but has to deal with the legacy of its predecessor, especially one that was in power for as long as the Conservatives had been. This legacy might be a benefit, as it clearly was in terms of the state of the economy, level of taxation and the control of public spending in 1997, but it can also be a liability in that a government, assuming it actually wants to carry out radical reforms, cannot stop providing services whilst it changes things: the 'year zero' option is not open to British politicians when it comes to reform.

But looking back and seeing what remains and why will also bring to light the disparity between rhetoric and action in New Labour. Looking at the extent of continuity that there is between New Labour and their Conservative predecessors will help us to see just what sort of government we have had since 1997. Just what is it about New Labour, or the circumstances in which it finds itself, that prevents it from creating policies all of its own or even going back to traditional Labour policies such as council house building? When we consider the policies prior to 1997 we see just how timid a government has been in power since 1997, one that seems only able to follow and not to lead, and this applies whether we are considering housing policy, the banning of fox hunting or even being led by the USA into war.

But stressing this continuity also allows us to deal with one of the oddest aspects of the last 7 years. This is the denial on the left that the current government is actually really rather conservative and thus it has not really made any difference at all. One frequently hears criticisms about New Labour housing policies, which end rather defiantly with the phrase, 'But at least it's not the Tories'. Indeed one does hear people state, with apparent sincerity, that New Labour stock transfer is actually different from Tory stock transfer, or people might argue that at least New Labour consults local authorities before imposing its restrictions on them. There is something of a desperate belief that New Labour really is different—*it just has to be*—apparently held by the majority of people who work in housing or comment on it. One, of course, can feel sorry for those whose political certainties are shot, but it is still necessary to deal with this delusion, and to state as clearly as possible what the level of continuity is and, more importantly, what that consensus is around: it is not on municipalism but ending council housing; it is not about extending social housing, but supporting owner occupation. One must assume that most people know this, but it is another thing to get them to admit it.

But this very sense of continuity works more in favour of New Labour than for the Conservative party, and so another aim of this book is to explore what effect this conservative consensus has for the future of conservatism. Whilst we can argue persuasively that the Conservatives would not have done much differently from New Labour, we also need to ask just what would they immediately change when or if they regained power again? The question, therefore, is what would be different under the Tories? What this suggests is that the Conservatives have very little to say on housing that cannot be immediately gainsaid by New Labour: what more could be done to support owner occupation or transfer social housing to the private sector? So unlike the late 1970s, when they took up the Right to Buy, the Conservatives do not appear to be able to use housing as a stepping stone to government. Those on the right, therefore, need to study the last twenty five years just as closely as those on the left.

Do Ideas Still Matter?

Perhaps what this shows is that thinking on housing is rather different from the traditional left/right split. This traditional, and hugely simplistic, analysis of the politics of housing associated owner occupation with the Conservatives and council housing with Labour. The priorities of the Conservative party were seen to be the development of individual choice, personal responsibility and independence, which can best be achieved through property ownership. Hence the Conservatives are associated with owner occupation, with their rhetorical support for the 'property owning democracy' and policies such as the Right to Buy. The Labour party in turn was associated with the growth of council housing and active government intervention, with a social agenda aimed at fostering solidarity and ensuring that society is organised as much for those at the bottom as at the top. To caricature, then, the Conservatives are the party of the market, while Labour is the party of the state.

This is indeed something of an oversimplification. The early labour movement may have initiated the debate on state subsidies to local authorities in the 1890s and the Labour party oversaw the massive expansion in public house building after World War Two. However, it was the Conservative governments between 1951 and 1964 that managed much of the expansion of council housing. Also whilst Labour can rightly be considered to be the party of public housing, senior Labour politicians can be found making supportive noises towards owner occupation as early as the late 1940s. We should therefore beware of stereotypes when we are considering the development of housing policy.

As an example of this, it was a commonplace to suggest that there was a consensus in housing policy from the later 1940s until 1979. The Conservative governments under Churchill, Eden and Macmillan continued with the expansion in public housing which began under Attlee's Labour administration. The consensus was continued through the 1960s and 1970s. But this too is something of an oversimplification. Whilst there were substantial areas of consensus, there were hard-fought disputes over issues such as the removal of rent controls in 1957 (Malpass, 1990) and the introduction of statutory provision for the homeless in 1977 (Richards, 1992). Thus the consensus might have been rather more noticeable in hindsight and once the divisions between the parties had become more marked after 1979.

Indeed the differences, manifested particularly over the implementation of the Right to Buy in 1980, were very real. The early 1980s saw a polarisation of political ideology and the dispute over housing tenure was a key area of dispute (Saunders, 1990). In some ways, this was a return to the position at the start of the twentieth century when the Conservatives were seen as the party of property, and Labour was closely associated with the inadequacy of working class housing. So one can point both to areas of real difference between the two parties, but also to periods in which policies converged, and we may now be in such as period of convergence. It may, however, necessitate our taking a step away from the action, so to speak, before we are able to recognise this.

One way of viewing the development of housing policy is as a series of dichotomies, as a dialectical progression where controversies are resolved and key departures made. In some ways this is the simplest and most convenient manner in which to see housing policy developing: this is because it separates us into opposing camps or ideological positions with entrenched views and ways of looking at the world. It allows us to see policy developments through particular prisms, and thus to link housing with important political and ideological movements and the clash of ideas.

But just how accurate is this way of perceiving housing? Is it not overly simplistic to see housing policy — or any complex area of public policy — as being centred round a binary opposition? More fundamentally still, is it not erroneous to view housing as being in any real sense ideological at all? Should we not take up the Third Way mantra, and see housing policy as a concern for 'what works'?

This way of looking at housing policy may have some superficial appeal, but it is my view that it would actually obscure more than it would enlighten. It seems to me that one of the main problems with housing is a lack of appreciation of the history of how we arrived at where we are now. We have become too concerned with current issues and problems to learn lessons from the past, and in consequence we risk the possibility of repeating the same mistakes again. The Blairite concern for 'modernisation' can and does quite easily lead to the disparagement of any consideration of the past. This is something we should remember when the apparent 'step change' promised in English housing provision (ODPM, 2003) is to be achieved in part through the use of off-site techniques which are generally considered to be expensive and are relatively untested. Should we not be worried when housing associations such as the Peabody Trust are criticised by the Audit Commission for being more concerned with innovative schemes such as the 'award-winning BedZED scheme in Sutton, North London, (which) cost £10m more than had been planned' (*Housing Today*, 14 May 2004, p. 9) than modernising their older properties? Are we not, in our rush to do things now, at risk of repeating the mistakes of the past? Indeed, is not looking back to the past a rather good way of finding out what works and what does not?

The Blair government is often criticised for its apparent ignorance of history: it is accused of discarding ancient traditions and institutions without appreciating their material and symbolic significance, and of promoting change and 'modernisation' for their own sakes. In response to this, the government claims it is dealing with new problems and has to respond to these in innovative ways. We are, they claim, now operating in a new paradigm, which demands a new form of politics. It thus appears to concur with its critics that it has little to learn from the past: it appears to believe that the problems it is facing are new ones.

In any case it is a particular conceit of policy makers and practitioners to dismiss the concerns of academics with the argument that they are too concerned with day-to-day issues — with immediate problems — and have no time to reflect on the past or on concepts and theories. But putting this less charitably, we can restate this as policy makers being too concerned with making their own mistakes to be concerned with the mistakes of the past!

But just how new are the problems facing government? As an example, the one constant of the last 25 years is the observation that 'housing is in crisis'. *The Housing Crisis* was the title of an excellent book from the mid 1980s (Malpass, 1986), yet one only has to read the current housing press to be confronted regularly with the notion of crisis and imminent disaster. Now, this might be because the problems are different, but a cursory look at Malpass's volume shows a concern for rent levels, overly limited public spending, the quality of the housing stock, and access. The cry, then as now, is for more investment, more affordable rents and effective means of dealing with homelessness and disrepair. So just what is new?

It is my view that *there really is nothing new to current problems*. One can suggest that the key issues in housing have always been about affordability, quality and access (King, 2001) and this applied to the nineteenth century public health acts, the early housing legislation in the 1920s, the *Housing (Homeless Persons) Act 1977* and the 2000 Housing Green Paper. It is these same basic issues that policy makers are grappling with; what differs are people's expectations and hence the acceptability of a range of solutions (King, 1998). What this suggests is that we can better understand our current problems by looking at how these same issues were dealt with in the past. The reason for this is that any current problems can be traced back to past policies which have developed in ways which were not intended and were unforeseen: current issues are often the result of past policy failure.

But as much as this book deals with history, so is it also concerned with ideology, and what effect this has had on housing policy. This concern for ideological development is important because we readily slip into cliché when considering policy. We use shorthand terms to create an impression and to suggest a meaning — 'social' as opposed to 'private', 'choice' as opposed to 'need' — and we do this because we know that these terms have a particular resonance. The mere attachment of the word 'private' conveys a particular image, conjuring up notions of profit, markets and a right-wing agenda. Conversely 'social' conveys the ideas of equality, fairness and justice. The significance of the Third Way and the appendage of the prefix 'New' to Labour is that the Blair government is trying to claim it has transcended these clichéd categories, and has found a means to combine the competitive nature of markets with social justice and equality.

Clearly, we have a choice as to whether we accept this transcendence or merely see New Labour and the Third Way as a chimera or a con trick — as 'global capitalism with a human face' (Žižek, 2000, p. 63)[2]. But what we need to do, *in either case*, is come to terms with what these ideological positions are, what impact they have had, and whether they still retain any relevance for the early twenty first century. If we can do this, then we might be able to understand what is at stake when New Labour claims to have reached a new synthesis. Put more simply, we might be able to determine whether there is anything new here or whether there is in fact a consensus built around long-standing conservative ideals.

It is not particularly my aim to see housing policy in Hegelian terms, as some sort of great dialectic process culminating in a unifying transcendence on 2 May 1997. I am not claiming, along with Fukuyama (1992), that we have reached 'the end of history', so that the current set of housing policies and tenure arrangements has been the purpose of past struggles[3]. Rather I am interested in exploring how far housing policy is a creature of ideology.

One cannot discuss modern housing policy without an appreciation of key ideological differences. So we cannot understand the significance that property ownership has, or is meant to play, in the lives of autonomous households without seeing that this has an ideological function. Similarly, the ownership of public assets such as council housing raises questions of the nature of the state and the manner in which it should provide for its citizens, and again this has an ideological import. These are all fundamental questions that, in

---

[2] Throughout this book I prefer to use New Labour rather than the 'Third Way'. This is largely because New Labour has almost entirely rejected the term and moved on to other justifications for its actions.

[3] As Fukuyama is always keen to reiterate, even as his critics seem equally disinclined to hear, his use of 'end' was intended to denote purpose and not closure.

their general import, have taxed thinkers since Plato and Aristotle. We should therefore not be surprised that a policy such as the Right to Buy, which involves both an extension of property ownership and an accusation of the stripping of public assets for private gain, divides politics and energises ideologues on both left and right. Policies, we should not forget, are the practical expression of ideas.

But politics is not as simple as this, of course. As I have suggested already, it is the case that any government, upon taking office, must start with what it is given in terms of the prevailing political institutions, economic conditions and policy instruments. Creating change takes time and, in democratic societies at least, must be undertaken gradually and through consent. This means that, whatever ideals one wishes to turn into practice, one can only proceed along predetermined paths and use already existing institutions, some of which may be the very antithesis of one's idea of good government. One might characterise this view by quoting the punch line to the bad joke about someone asking directions to Dublin: 'If I were you I wouldn't start from here'. The point of the joke is precisely that we do have to start from *here*. This might be a difficult spot, and getting out of it might be our priority, but we cannot ignore the fact that we are there. Moreover, understanding how we got there might prove to be of some use to us, particularly so that we can learn how not to end up there again. The important point is that we cannot wish away the journey up to the point where we got lost and sought directions.

Policy makers have to start with the institutions, resources, and policies that they inherit. But because they have to reform existing institutions this means they come up against vested interests, traditional ways of operating, and precedents. It is noticeable that those who defend both the NHS and council housing rely on the historical purpose of these institutions. Likewise, it is not coincidental that the Thatcher government did not attempt any serious welfare reforms until their third term (1987 onwards), nor that the Blair government is criticised for its slow progress on reform.

This situation being so, we can pick out a dichotomy in policy between pragmatism on the one hand, and radicalism on the other. We might describe this as the choice between vision and managerialism. The dichotomy is between those who seek rapid and fundamental change, and those who wish to work with current institutions and amend them slowly, ensuring there is no great disruption and upset. Hills (1991) has described housing policy as a cat's cradle, a complex interweaving of threads where the connections and inter-dependencies are not immediately obvious. We might be tempted to pull hard, but doing so is just as likely to create a mess, which we will then struggle to sort out. But on the other hand, there are those who contend that unless we act quickly and decisively, we risk being compromised by existing vested interests. If we want fundamental change this can be done better by 'shock therapy' rather than gradual change (Skidelsky, 1995). After all, if current institutions are the problem, why should we expect that we can use them to achieve our ends?

Of course, all this assumes that political parties act in a consistent manner and do not change from the route (and roots!) they are assumed to have. But, as appeared to be the case in the 1990s, there may be a disjuncture between a party's current and historical position. As Giddens (1994) has pointed out, the party of radicalism, Labour, and its allies in the trade unions, found themselves on the defensive in the face of an onslaught from a radical right-wing government. It was those on the left who were trying to preserve its traditional liberties and institutions. They were the reactionaries and the Conservatives were the radicals. Giddens (1994) therefore talks of a *philosophical conservatism*, where one has a general, perhaps time-limited, disposition against change. This disposition, he argues, has little to do with one's expressed ideology, but more to do with the prevailing political circumstances. Accordingly, the old guard of the Soviet communist party were the reactionaries, and free market politicians such as Yeltsin the radicals. This is an issue of considerable importance to the argument of this book and one that I return to at some length: indeed this entire book might be seen as a discussion on the consistency, or otherwise of assumed ideological positions.

Yet the question remains as to the actual role that ideology plays in policy development. Does ideology play much of a role at all, or is it more the case that the fine grain of policy is not determined by big ideas but more mundane matters? How far is politics about expediency and how much is down to principle? As it is quite rare for parties to split and for new alliances to form, we need to try to understand what connection there is between ideology and pragmatism, and how this relates to the essentially tribal nature of politics. At issue here is again the question of whether we should be concerned with ideology or with party.

One way of tackling all these questions at once is to suggest that ideology creates the framework in which more detailed policy making sits. So, we can separate the principled decision to implement a massive council house building programme in the late 1940s from the detailed subsidy mechanisms used. Clearly there is a relation between the two, but the principle need not entirely depend on particular mechanisms. Likewise, the Right to Buy was based on an ideological presupposition, but the guidance developed to implement it and deal with the resulting capital receipts was not cast in stone as a result. One way of seeing this distinction might be that of ends and means: a government wishes to achieve certain ideological ends and then has to determine particular means to achieve them. It may choose radical means if these appear appropriate or feasible, or it might choose a more pragmatic tack. This may be a simplification of the political process (for instance, can ends and means really be separated?) but it might offer us a way of locating the significance of ideology and where its limits might be.

The importance of this discussion is that it raises the difficult, but crucial, issue of *continuity*. Perhaps like all governments, the Blair government claimed that perdition ended and heavenly virtue began only when they were elected in May 1997. Hence, as we have already seen, the 2000 Housing Green Paper with its emphasis on choice was called the first comprehensive review of housing policy for twenty three years. This conveniently sidetracked such significant policies as the Right to Buy and the fact that choice had also featured heavily in Conservative Housing White Papers in 1987 and 1995 (DOE, 1987, 1995). We might suggest that the idea of choice has been at the heart of housing policy since the mid 1980s, and what the Blair government has tried to do is to re-invent it as its 'big idea', when, in fact, it is merely continuing, or at best extending, the policies of its predecessors.

The problem for us here, however, is whether this is precisely what we should see New Labour as being about — that it is meant to be an ideological magpie — or whether this shows that politics is as much about opportunism and populism as principles. Of course, the answer we would give to this question would itself be coloured by ideology. It would depend on what we thought of the New Labour project. Accordingly, most of its critics are those who oppose its post-ideological position and who instead sit in what might be called the 'Old Left' or 'New Right' corners. This means, perhaps unsurprisingly, that we can only understand the criticisms of New Labour when we appreciate the ideological baggage they bring to the argument.

As should now be apparent, there is a considerable degree of circularity here: ideology is important to policy making precisely because we hold our ideologies to be important, and they thus determine how we contend with debates on policy. But this is because, for most of us, it is our ideological position—our fundamental beliefs—that tells us 'what works'. There is therefore no necessary opposition between continuity and ideology. What differs are the means by which we seek to achieve our ends, and consequently how near or far we are from those who oppose us. Sometimes the gulf is large and the policy debate is both deep and acrimonious, whilst on other occasions we can see a consensus. This is always a matter of degree, but ideology is always a matter of importance. This is because it can tell where we are, and, more importantly in this case, where others are. An understanding of the importance of ideology, therefore, can tell us much about what certain policies mean. This book, then, is essentially a study of ideology, and in particular the conservative ideology as it manifests itself in modern British, or more particularly, English politics. More particularly still, it is a study of the impact of the conservative ideology on English housing policy. And this connection between conservatism and housing is a peculiar one.

The Way We Use Our Housing

It is my contention that what matters most of all in this discussion on housing and ideology is the manner in which we use our housing. Only once we understand the role that housing plays at the personal, and therefore non-political, level, can we come to terms with how and why a consensus has developed over housing policy, and how this has been modelled by conservative ideology.

As ordinary members of the public we like to think that elections matter, or else why do we have them? Politicians, being primarily tribal, would also tend to say that elections matter, and, in the sense of handing the keys to power over to one group rather than another, they certainly do count. Moreover, they do matter regardless of the number of people who vote in them: New Labour does not have less power because they won in 2005 with only 10 million votes compared with the 14 million garnered by the Conservatives in 1992.

But also most politicians tend to be risk averse, and this applies regardless of the size of their majority or popular vote. Modern politicians tend to stick with the popular and back away from the risky and the dangerous. The main principle is of 'safety first' and indeed what happens when they do take risks is illuminating: does Blair really relish being remembered for the ill-advised adventurism that led to the quagmire of Iraq? Likewise, Thatcher is as much remembered for the Poll Tax and the Euro as any of her policy successes. Hence we can claim that caution has some merit to it.

Of course, this innate caution might not be matched by the rhetoric. Thatcher claimed that she was 'not for turning' and gave the impression that she was resolute and determined. However, her record shows considerably more caution, with a piecemeal approach taken to both privatisation and trade union reform. As with the miners' strike, she was astute at choosing the time and place for her battles[4]. Likewise, New Labour is full of a rhetoric of 'modernisation'. When we look at their housing policies we hear lots of talk about 'step-changes' and 'transformation': New Labour does not just build houses but 'creates sustainable communities', as well as ensuring that all homes are 'decent'. Their rhetoric is all about shifting to a higher gear, dealing with backlogs, and bringing in new initiatives and actions, all of which are 'joined-up' and 'modern'. We see targets and inspections and the drive to efficiency, with lots of pseudo-business jargon thrown in.

And yet I would suggest that what all this activity turns on is *property ownership*. For all the clamour about strategic planning and best practice, New Labour's record on spending and house building does not bear up well with any of its predecessors, with spending in their second term at a third in real terms of spending in 1980/81, and public sector housing completions declining every year from 1997 until 2003 (Wilcox, 2004). In 1980 110,000 social housing dwellings were built compared with 18,279 in 2003. It will need to be quite a step-change.

Social housing policy does not match the rhetoric which supports it, and this is because it does not actually matter to our current crop of risk averse politicians. What does concern these politicians is home ownership, and this is because this is what matters most to the public. In fact the public's concern is even more specific: they are not so much concerned with owner occupation as the particular house that they own and what they can do with it.

The majority of households are owner occupiers. What concerns this majority is issues such as the choices they can make, and how their dwelling affects them materially. This sense of ownership

---

[4] Of course, as Blair is finding to his cost, it actually helps you to appear resolute if you win the wars you start.

brings with it a feeling of affluence and a sense of independence so that one is not reliant on government. Owning our own dwelling allows us to ignore politicians, and to insulate ourselves from their boasts and hubristic noises, so that we really do begin to feel that perhaps elections do not matter after all: why bother with the ballot box when we are sovereign consumers? As consumers we can make choices that directly affect us on a daily basis and not just every 4–5 years. In this sense, it is our income and our property that enfranchise us. Accordingly, we can ignore politicians with impunity, or perhaps we have become immune to their arguments and pleadings.

I want to assert that the preponderance of owner occupation has had a considerable effect on politics and that has led to an ideological transformation. It is this which creates the conservative consensus I have claimed is present. What is important is that it is owner occupation which has created this ideological shift, and not the ideology which created the support for owner occupation. First, as owner occupiers we have become sceptical about what government can do for us. We want it to be cautious and in the background. We do not want to be nannied by politicians and we will seek to punish them when they try. We do indeed have 'a stake in the system', and this does not just make us rather more conservative, but also we begin to insist that our governments act conservatively. Second, we have come to relish having choices, and to have a sense that we are in control. We therefore feel that government can leave us alone as far as our housing is concerned (with the corollary that we want government to step in when we feel we cannot control our surroundings, and hence we want action on the fear of crime, health scares and so on). Third, we now quite naturally see property ownership as a good thing in itself: we enjoy the security it can give us and our children. In short, we feel that property ownership is natural.

What I want to suggest is that the attitude towards owner occupation is one of the main ways in which the conservative disposition is manifested. I shall, of course, spend a considerable amount of time in the first part of the book discussing what this disposition is, but for the moment I shall describe it simply as an important need that we have *to hold dear those things that are close to us*. It is the sense that we are made by our relations to those things that are around us, our family, our immediate belongings, our home, and that on and through these are founded our relations with others.

This disposition, as we shall see, is a peculiar form of ideology, one that is reactive and which does not act in the form of programmatical statements starting 'I believe ...' Rather we should see it as an attitude or even a practice, such that we live it out rather than declare it. It is in this way that our use of our dwelling is so instructive. But the conservative ideology is also peculiar in that it is not in essence political at all. It is rather inchoate, being an unarticulated series of habits and attitudes rather than anything with a slogan or banner attached. This diminishes its visibility, but not its profundity or its influence. What this means is that it is for politics to respond to the disposition: politics can help or hinder it, but not create it. It is formed outside politics and increasingly in the home.

Despite what many will and do think of conservatism, I do not consider the disposition I articulate here as being particularly reprehensible. Of course, there is much more to life than property and wealth; it is just that most of those other things only become possible if we have a place to live and some disposable income. The fault would be to see owner occupation as an end in itself, just as it would be an error to see an ideology as something that exists merely for itself. The reason that Marxism has ceased to operate as a serious idea is that it was found to be murderous. Accordingly, the test for the conservative disposition is what it does in people's lives and what it says about how they do and should live. What is different about it, certainly compared to Marxism, is that it derives not from any utopian sense of what society could or should be like, but rather from the manner in which we do things, such as how we live and spend our money. It is grounded in quotidian practices and in the things that we use to give our lives, as they currently are, their sense of meaning. This is certainly rather more mundane than building barricades and making speeches exhorting others to action, but at least it is safer.

Structure of the Book

This book is structured to go from the general to the specific and then back again, in that it begins with a consideration of ideology, moves on to a discussion of housing policy and then back to ideology again. Chapter one considers the conservative disposition, and offers a detailed discussion of what conservatism is and how it links to, and differs from, the Conservative party. In chapter two I move on to look at libertarianism to assess what influence these ideas have had on Conservative politics in the 1980s and 1990s. I suggest that, broadly speaking, the similarities between the two ideologies outweigh their differences, but that conservatism was able to absorb libertarianism without fundamentally altering itself. Chapter three then considers the actual impact that ideology had and whether this was tempered by pragmatism. The argument of this chapter is that, as a key part of the conservative disposition is pragmatism or gradualism, this too can be accommodated without any difficulty.

Chapter four moves on to policy and considers Conservative housing, making the links between the ideology and particular policies such as the Right to Buy and the use of private finance. This chapter does not restrict itself to the 1979 to 1997 period, although much of the discussion centres on it. Chapter five moves the story on to a consideration of post-1997 housing policies. The considerable degree of continuity is shown and any differences of emphasis discussed. Chapter six moves back to a discussion of ideology by considering the nature of New Labour and whether it has any substance independent of its predecessor's policies. This chapter also undertakes a critique of the language of New Labour, which might be used to hide a lack of substance. The conclusion considers the nature of the conservative consensus after nearly a decade of the Blair government, and what future the success of New Labour might mean for the Conservatives as well as the conservative disposition.

As should be clear this book takes a broadly sympathetic view of conservatism if not necessarily the Conservative party. I am generally critical of New Labour despite the fact that they are following a broadly conservative path. This, as far as I can tell, makes the book unique, in that there has been virtually no sympathetic assessment of Conservative housing policies and their impact on New Labour. This, of course, does not make my argument any better or worse. However, it does, I hope, offer a distinctly different view that opens up housing discourse into new areas. I hope that any conservatives who do read this do not object to my attempts at originality: it is not, I know, a very conservative thing to do.

Chapter One
Conservatism

Conservatism, it is often said, is somewhat different from other political ideologies. Indeed, we might see that it is not really an ideology at all. Now this is, of course, a dangerous track to take. Both Marxists and classical liberals have suggested that their positions are criticisms of ideology, and that *they* are immune to the vice of ideology themselves. We can suggest that this is both a convenient position and an unconvincing one. Both Marxism and classical liberalism are normative social theories seeking to justify a particular form of social organisation. They are, to use the definition of Adams (1993), a set of beliefs that one accepts and uses to justify one's actions. These beliefs rest on some normative principles which cannot be gainsaid or further underpinned. What they are not is a science or rational critique that stands above or beyond the cut and thrust of belief and opinion.

With this in mind, I do not want to suggest that conservatism is not an ideology. There is a set of beliefs which can generally be referred to as conservatism, even if these are rather broad. But, as we shall see, these beliefs are somewhat different in type from those held by other ideologies. Therefore, it is not merely that conservatives believe in different things from Marxists or liberals, but it is rather a matter of ambition and scope. Unlike other ideologies, including libertarianism or classical liberalism that it is sometimes associated with, conservatism is not necessarily concerned with ends, but rather with processes. It is an ideology concerned with means. It does not have a particular end, other than that of good government. Accordingly, conservatism is wary of the notion of abstract theorising, of the universal statement of where a particular society ought to be if it is to be called 'good'. As Quinton (1993) states, 'As an ideology conservatism is, then, procedural or methodological rather than substantive. It prescribes no principles or ideals or institutions universally and so falls outside the scope of its own rejection of abstract theory' (p. 247). Conservative ideology therefore presents no model for how society should look, rather it is concerned with the means by which change both occurs and can be managed. Conservatism, indeed, involves a critique of abstraction and concerns itself instead with the means by which a society might thrive. In this way it is distinctly different from all other political ideologies which will usually assert a series of ends based on a series of specific principles.

The critics of conservatism will claim, no doubt, that this attempt to differentiate between conservatism and other ideologies is mere hedging around the issue of ideology, and is consequently just a means of claiming the same 'distinctive' status as Marxism and classical liberalism. However, I hope to show that this is not the case, and that there really is a difference between conservatism and other ideologies. Where we shall find difficulties is in associating this disposition with *actually existing conservatism*, particularly in the form of the UK Conservative party.

But before commencing this discussion I would like to draw an interesting parallel between this view of conservative ideology and post 1997 UK politics. As I have implied in the introduction, a shorthand means of describing the methodological basis of conservative ideology would be to state that it concentrates on 'what works'. It is a form of particularism married to pragmatism, which treats issues on a case by case basis and attempts piecemeal solutions to problems. Of course, it is precisely by using this slogan that New Labour attempted to sell its Third Way ideology (Brown, 1999). The Third Way, we were told, was about doing what works rather than basing policies on predetermined ideologies. We shall consider New Labour and its coherence later in this book, but this emphasis on the pragmatic does raise an interesting, if rather speculative, point. We tend to see ideologies as operating at the political level. They are ways of thinking that individuals and groups have, which give them an apparatus with which to engage in political debates and with political institutions. These ideologies may cover a reasonable range of ideas and approaches, and thus allow for differences between individuals and within groups.

Yet might we not see conservatism as operating differently? If conservatism is as we will describe it — as a disposition based on a sense of procedure — we might suggest that it operates at three levels. First, individuals can be disposed towards conservatism, seeking to maintain their current position and defend what they hold dear. Thus apparently radical trade unionists might be better characterised as demonstrating a conservative disposition. This might not be a particularly political outlook: for instance we can see this disposition in certain parts of the Anglican Church, particularly in opposition to issues such as women and homosexual priests. However, as O'Hara (2005) states, this idea of what Giddens (1994) has referred to as philosophical conservatism, is little more than reaction. O'Hara argues that we cannot reduce conservatism merely to the opposition to change and the protection of vested interests. Indeed were we to take this line of reasoning, we would be forced to state that nearly every politician, every party and every institution was conservative almost by definition. Whilst, there is certainly some interest in suggesting that people and institutions have a natural desire to preserve themselves, and thus react negatively to change, this should not be equated with conservatism.

Second, we can see conservatism as referring to actual policies and practices that are conservative. These we will often refer to as Conservative or Tory, giving a proper name to these policies and practices to place them in a particular historical and cultural context. Hence we can, and will, discuss the policies of the UK Conservative party as a distinctive entity. There is a difficulty here, of course, in that some policies adopted by the Labour party might be considered conservative (for example, supports to owner occupation, the Private Finance Initiative, and so on). Indeed, some policies which are pursued by the Conservatives in the UK might also be pursued by the Democratic party in the USA (for example, welfare reform such as workfare). It might even be that some of the policies pursued by the Conservative party are not particularly conservative, for example, the enforced abolition of grammar schools by the Heath government in the 1970s. What is important here, though, is that it is possible to see conservatism as being a tribal connection, or almost a defining label, so that one is a conservative because of one's membership of the Tory party.

Third, we might see this conservative disposition as existing throughout a culture, where there is a general disposition towards tradition and recourse to established institutions and past precedent to influence the present. This might coincide roughly with Weber's notion of political legitimacy being based on tradition rather than bureaucracy or charisma (Quinton, 1993). What this suggests is that certain countries have political and cultural traditions that might be described as conservative, and all political parties seeking influence within that country must operate according to those restrictions, and this would apply regardless of the government in power and whether it considered itself in the least bit conservative. Clearly, this takes us beyond political ideology as such, and into the realms of political psychology and whether there is any such thing as national character (which, as we shall see, is a conservative idea in itself). However, my speculation is that British political culture is conservative and therefore all political parties need — and want — to operate within this particular atmosphere. We should not therefore be surprised if New Labour, despite its rhetoric of modernism and boasts of 'step-changes', is actually merely another manifestation of what we might call a *meta-ideology*, or better, a *cultural condition of politics*.

New Labour operates within a political culture it has not created and can only seek to influence slowly. The slogan of doing 'what works' might then be best seen as an attempt to connect with a deep-seated disposition towards particularism and pragmatism. But then we might also say that this is merely what every other government before New Labour has sought to do as well. The British electorate would not take kindly to a prospective government placing ideology above common sense, of forcing things upon them regardless of whether these things work or not.

Many will find the notion that we have a conservative political culture objectionable, and would doubtless point to the elections in 1997, 2001 and 2005 for support. But we need to appreciate that the differences between political parties in the UK are relatively minor. The disputes between them are on specifics, which of themselves may cause considerable controversy and argument, yet all parties accept the established procedures of politics. The means by which politics is done in Britain is established as a gradualist, piecemeal approach to change, all based on an understanding of the pluralism of ends. As we shall see, this is essentially a conservative approach, even if many of these changes are controversial and contested (not least by the Conservative party itself).

The problem that many commentators will have in accepting this position is that the majority of them see the current political settlement as contingent. That is to say, they see the political structures in the UK as illegitimate and ripe for transformation, typically into some form of socialist state in which capitalist institutions are abolished or at least seriously contained. Many commentators on housing and social policy see the political spectrum as being much wider than is actually the case in practice, if we were to see electability and public support as the main criteria. The academy still has many radicals and revolutionaries amongst its number, and whilst they are safer there than in the real world, this does colour their approach to policy issues. What they are testing policies against are not the practicalities that concern elected politicians, but an abstract ideological position in which purity is seen as more important than applicability. But conservatism, to reiterate, is not an abstract ideological position, but rather it is an engaged one. Moreover, it is engaged in the means of politics rather than the ends.

In this chapter I wish to build a convincing case to support this speculation about the nature of politics. I begin with some broad definitions, which offer a general sense of the ideology, but which also link into the last point about the pervasiveness of conservatism within an entire culture. Having done this I wish to concentrate on one particular element of conservatism, seen by many, be they friends or enemies, as its defining characteristic. This is the support for the principle of property ownership. This, we shall see, is central to any definition of conservatism. But it also allows for the discussion to be expanded to consider more fully the link between Conservatism — as that which the Conservative party does — and libertarianism. We have to take seriously the libertarian (or classical liberal) cast to Thatcherism and Conservative politics in the 1980s and 1990s as this was undoubtedly of some influence: both Mrs Thatcher and Sir Keith Joseph entreated colleagues and civil servants to read Hayek's *The Constitution of Liberty* (Hayek, 1960), although, as Ebenstein (2001) states, Hayek saw no evidence that Mrs Thatcher had read the book herself. In chapter two, therefore, I consider the influence of libertarianism and seek to judge the relative influence of this more assertive ideology against the more dispositional approach I discuss in this chapter. Having done this I want then to contend more fully with the view I have touched on already, namely that of ideological purity, and more particularly whether policy is determined more by pragmatism — 'what works' — rather than ideology. Hence, chapter three deals with whether we can reconcile this discussion of ideology to the actual practice of politics.

As should be clear already in this discussion, my view is that we can point to some specific entity called conservatism, and that this is something distinct of itself, even if it might be influenced by the 'alien' ideology of libertarianism. Moreover, one of the characteristics of conservatism is that it is inherently pragmatic, and this relates back to its dispositional quality and the emphasis of means and not ends. The strength of conservatism, therefore, is that it is as much cultural as political. However, I am getting ahead of myself and need to return to the start and define what I believe conservatism to be.

Defining Conservatism

When we consider recent Conservative governments, particularly those led by Mrs. Thatcher, the terms that most readily spring to mind are those such as 'radical', 'divisive', 'committed' and 'controversial'. These governments were noted for their activism, their strong sense of purpose and sense of direction. We might disagree with that direction and see them as seriously misguided, but they were certainly purposive. From this we might want to suggest that conservatism is about strong actions and committed and purposeful leadership. Yet in many ways conservatism appears to stand for the opposite. It is not about ends, but is rather concerned with means. It does not stand for any clearly articulated set of principles.

In trying to deal with this apparent paradox, Giddens (1994) talks of a shift in the nomenclature of politics. Those on the right, such as Thatcher and Reagan (and we can add the second President Bush to this list), became the radicals, eager to force through change, often against the will of established interests and institutions. Against this he suggests that parties and agencies who were erstwhile noted for their radicalism, such as the British trade union movement, environmentalists and Eastern European communists, were now acting like reactionaries who sought to prevent or halt change. This leads Giddens to posit the concept of philosophical conservatism. This he sees as a general presumption against change, and a belief that current institutions need preserving. It is just that the institutions apparently in danger are those of the traditional left such as trade union rights, state control and environmental controls. It was the post war settlement that appeared to be under threat by the Thatcher governments and thus 'radical politics' — as traditionally defined — became more about reacting to threats and protecting institutions than transforming society. We have already suggested, along with O'Hara (2005), that this is not really conservatism but simply a reaction to threats. However, it does indicate that we cannot simply assume that conservatism is simply a reaction to any change.

Of course, what Thatcherites might well argue is that radical and controversial changes were necessary in order to *preserve* something important: that the only manner in which society could be returned to its proper — conservative — nature was through changes that would appear divisive to many. This argument is familiar to conservatives since Burke (1999), who saw change as necessary, but as a means of preserving and maintaining those institutions we hold dear.

I shall deal more with this apparent radicalism of Thatcherism in chapter two when I consider whether there was any libertarian influence on the Conservative governments of the 1980s and 1990s. However, what I find interesting about Giddens's idea of philosophical conservatism is that he sees it not as a defined set of doctrines or dogma — it is not a political programme — but as an *attitude*, or a way in which individuals and groups are predisposed to respond to threats to their perceived interests. Even though we might want to dispense with Giddens's conclusions that trade unionists and environmentalists are in some way demonstrating conservatism, we need to admit that this notion of an attitude is precisely how conservative thinkers themselves would characterise their beliefs. Giddens, in this sense, has picked up on something elemental to conservatism even as he has then gone on to misuse it.

Most writers on conservatism do not see it as a theory of society but as a *disposition*. It is a way of thinking and acting or having an attitude, which predisposes us towards certain responses. Hence Kirk (1985) can talk of *The Conservative Mind*, rather than a set of theories or a description of a utopia[1]. Fundamentally, conservatives like Kirk believe they are merely recognising and responding to how human beings are. And if Giddens is not prepared to go this far, he at least appears to recognise it as a disposition that, in some circumstances and on some occasions, even supposed radicals can be prey to.

But we still have not done any more than hint at what conservatism consists of: we need to be more specific. The problem in doing this though lies precisely in the fact that conservatism is not a set of doctrines. Indeed, as Scruton (2001) argues, it is seldom explicitly articulated by its adherents. He suggests that at one level we should not expect advocates of moderation or a 'middle way' to feel the need to articulate their views. Advocates of 'keeping things as there are' would quite naturally find themselves at a loss to explain why things should be this way. The adherents of conservatism, seen as a general complacency with how things are and the concomitant reluctance to contemplate a movement away from the status quo,

---

[1] Indeed Kirk does not depend on political thought and thinkers for his discussion preferring to rely on writers like Fennimore Cooper, Macaulay, Carlyle, Scott and Eliot.

would find their position a self-evident one. Scruton states that conservatism 'is characteristically inarticulate, unwilling (and indeed usually unable) to translate itself into formulae or maxims, loath to state its purpose or declare its view' (p. 9).

But this does not mean that we should not try to define conservatism, nor that others have not tried to do so. The simplest definition would be to suggest that conservatives seek to *conserve*: they aim to keep things as they are. But, quite rightly, Scruton feels that to state that conservatives have a desire to conserve is a rather limp definition. Unlike Giddens's notion of philosophical conservatism, what needs to be considered is what is to be conserved and why (O'Hara, 2005). It is not enough simply to say that we wish to conserve. We must qualify this by stating what we wish to maintain and why it is so important for us to do so.

What we are aiming to conserve are those things close to us and which we hold dear. So, for Scruton, 'conservatism arises indirectly from the sense that one belongs to some continuing, and pre-existing social order, and that this fact is all-important in determining what to do' (2001, p. 10). We feel ourselves to be part of some larger whole, which defines us as individuals. This social entity becomes mingled with the private lives of its members: 'They may feel in themselves the persistence of the will that surrounds them. The conservative instinct is founded in that feeling: it is the enactment of historical vitality, the individual's sense of the society's will to live' (Scruton, 2001, p. 10). Expressed in this manner we can see why it might be unarticulated. Scruton sees it almost as a gut reaction, as something elemental[2]. Conservatism is about the relationship we have with those things around us, and in particular here with those social entities that form us and which we therefore identify with as defining of our sense of self. As we shall see when we discuss Scruton's ideas on property and owning things, there is more than a hint of Hegelian idealism in this most English of conservatives. Scruton's connection between individual and social life appears to owe much to Hegel's conception of freedom as consecrated in the bond between individual and society, where we are only free to act because we are located within a social whole (Hegel, 1991).

Already at this stage, we can see that conservatism has little or nothing to do with individualism: individuals are defined in relation to something else, rather than the liberal view whereby individuals

---

[2] But we should also note that Scruton's language, in all its elegance, is not that of the saloon bar. He is very far from the inarticulate conservative.

are complete in themselves and where their qualities come, as it were, from within. Conservatives do not subscribe to the Kantian ideal of individuals being ends rather than means. This is not because they are against freedom of the individual, but rather they believe that one cannot be free unless one is surrounded by some set of social relations that allow one to operate. The important thing though is that conservatives look to things outside of themselves to define them as individuals: they are not sufficient unto themselves, but rely on social institutions and collective notions to sustain them. A conservative view of the individual therefore appears diametrically opposed to a libertarian view.

Scruton sees the conservative instinct deriving from a need to feel connected to some pre-existing social order, and from a need to protect this sense of belonging. We can explore this further by trying to understand what conservatives might mean by this sense of pre-existence and continuity. Quinton (1993) suggests that there are three central elements in conservative thought: *traditionalism, scepticism* and *organicism*. These are all connected to this sense of continuity, but also inform us as to when and why change is necessary and acceptable, and how it should be attempted.

Traditionalism

This first element relates most directly to the rather simplistic view of conservatism as being about 'conserving' and reaction to change. Quinton suggests that traditionalism is based on a support for continuity in politics, for the maintenance of existing institutions and practices, and a suspicion of change. Where change is seen as necessary, it should be gradual and only undertaken after careful consideration: it should be evolutionary and piecemeal rather than fundamental and transforming. The ideal for a conservative would be a situation where change comes only in response to extra-political circumstances such as population changes. The political arrangements of a community are, for the conservative, settled and permanent.

But the support for traditionalism does not derive merely from reactionary instincts or inertia (although there may be some of this), but from the instrumental effects of these long-standing practices and institutions. It is presumed that these would not have existed for so long without providing some considerable benefit to our ancestors and ourselves. Accordingly, Kekes (1998) identifies a conservative traditionalism that protects those institutions that allow individual autonomy to flourish. This tradition implies the limiting of government's authority to interfere with these institutions. He sees a predisposition to institutional arrangements that promote individual autonomy and that the conservation of tradition serves to embed this sense of liberty. One such institution, of course, is private property rights, but we might also point to the rule of law and the mechanisms that ensure its enforcement.

Perhaps the most famous and elegant discussion of the virtue of traditions is that of Burke (1999), who stated that society is a partnership between the living, the dead and those yet to be born. A society is based on inherited patterns and traditions and the living have a duty to respect the interests of the dead and the unborn. This is because these patterns and traditions embody the interests of the dead and offer a prospectus to the unborn. One respects the dead by preserving and passing on what they have created to those yet to come. Thus social institutions are not *ours*, but held in trust for future generations. This statement of Burke's is also important in its realisation of the organic nature of a society, a doctrine we shall consider below.

In justifying traditionalism Quinton offers a number of arguments used by conservatives. First, they cite the effects of unintended consequences, those outcomes of political action that were not, and could not, have been predicted by the actors involved. Changes in one part of the political realm may have consequences that were unforeseen and indeed ripple out to the extent that the repercussions may go considerably beyond the political realm. Of course, unintended consequences need not necessarily be negative — change can have positive results. However, it is the sheer unpredictability of change that causes concern for conservatives. If we are unable to predict outcomes with any certainty, how can we rationally propose change? The issue is merely compounded by the fact that the current situation is known — we are aware of what existing institutions offer us, with all their imperfections — whereas the future is always hypothetical. Those with a utopian cast of mind would, of course, see the opposite possibility here, where the future is untainted by the ugly, imperfect present, but for a conservative this is mere wishful thinking. The conservative disposition is very much tied to the present, and if it is looking anywhere it is backwards. So where change is seen as necessary, it should be planned and gradual to ensure that any unplanned effects can be understood and, where necessary (and possible), countermanded. According to Scruton, in order to minimise the dangers involved, change should be continuous and gradual. So conservatism does not mean a rejection of change: 'The desire to conserve is compatible with all manner of change, provided only that change is also continuity' (Scruton, 2001, p. 11).

This fear of the unexpected is compounded by a second justification for traditions, which Quinton refers to as the 'tightrope approach' to politics. This is the essentially pessimistic position that there are many ways in which change can go wrong, but only very few ways of getting it right. Decision makers are balancing on a very fine line indeed, and the spaces either side are cavernous and dangerous. This attitude leads to two consequences. The first is that if change is so difficult and potentially dangerous, we should take great care in how we undertake it. We should make sure we are properly prepared (the rope is securely attached, we have the right equipment, and the weather conditions are not adverse). Second, we should leave the crossing of tightropes to the experts. The difficulties involved are such that we should not expect all to be able to manage it. Indeed only very few will have the talents, skills and experience to get from one side to the other intact.

The third justification is empirical, in that conservatives can point to many historical examples of bad changes, which have led to political upheaval, mass murder and even genocide. Since Burke's time in the late eighteenth century, conservatives have warned against the effect of utopian adventure in politics. From the conservative point of view, there have been far too many examples of bad changes to make anything acceptable other than changes which are piecemeal, controlled and evolutionary. This element of traditionalism links into another key doctrine associated with conservatism, namely a sceptical view of political knowledge.

But before looking at this second doctrine, I wish to consider the main criticism of traditionalism. Critics argue that the problem with traditionalism is that it opposed things which we now all accept, universal suffrage for instance. Hayek, in his famous essay *Why I am not a Conservative* (1960), contends that there is some inconsistency and incoherence in this traditionalist strand of conservatism. It is inconsistent, in that is seeks to prevent further change, but not past change that has created the current political settlement. Universal suffrage is now accepted, but changes such as the abolition of hereditary peers and the introduction of regional government are opposed for breaking long-standing traditional and local ties. Hayek sees that the problem is as if dynamic societies should stop at some point which is to the liking of conservative thinkers. Of course, what this leads to is a succession of conservatives saying 'this much and no more'. But in previous generations conservatives opposed what their successors now accept. Modern conservatives accept democracy and popular sovereignty as a matter of course, but past conservatives found this notion thoroughly dangerous. Thus conservatism is seen as incoherent in that it deals with social change differently depending on when it occurred: past change is (now) good, but any further change is bad.

But Quinton argues that there is no real inconsistency here, as the high social costs of these changes have now been paid. We therefore quite rationally see the past, which is settled, as different from the future, which is still to be made. Also the social costs of change might well have been lighter if the conservatives' call for gradual change had been listened to at the time. But, in any case, these things are now part of the customary established political order and have to be accepted as such. This response by Quinton is pragmatic and practical, but does not deal with Hayek's objection that conservatism is illogical, in that these changes, which conservatives now accept, would never have come about if they had been listened to at the time. This problem is recognised, in part at least, by Scruton in his book *England: An Elegy* (2000), and it is the subtitle of the book that is important here. Scruton looks back to an idea (ideal?) of England in the 1950s and before, which he sees as breaking down under the weight of social reform, the Americanisation of popular culture, and European integration. But he is also aware that it is neither possible nor necessarily desirable to turn the clock back to this apparent golden age. Change is often only a one-way process, and we cannot undo what we have done and unlearn what we now know. Therefore, for Scruton, the function of the conservative becomes one of elegy, of reminding their fellow citizens of their inheritance and what it means to be in the here and now. Indeed conservatives must make others aware that the 'here and now' is built on certain foundations and there are consequences to altering those foundations without proper thought. The role of the conservative is to put a restraint on change in order to ensure that it is properly thought through and is consistent with the traditions and customs which have developed over time.

Scepticism

The second key element of conservatism identified by Quinton (1993) is scepticism about political knowledge. This arises out of a traditional world view and also colours the conservative attitude to social change. Quinton argues:

> Political wisdom ... is embodied ... in the inherited fabric of established laws and institutions. This is seen as the deposit of a great historical accumulation of small adjustments to the political order made by experienced practitioners, acting under the pressure of a clearly recognised need in a cautious, prudent way (1993, p. 245).

Political wisdom is the accrual of very many tiny adjustments in the political realm. Politicians are seen as operating under the pressure of events, using their accumulated judgements to minimise the adverse consequences of these pressures, and to protect the essential elements within the political fabric. Politics is seen as being responsive and defensive rather than programmatic.

A sceptical attitude is seen as necessary because there are clear limits to what we can know about the political realm. Kekes (1998) suggests that conservatives are sceptical because, whilst we might seek to base political arrangements on a rational basis, there are distinct limits to reason. Conservatives, according to Kekes, do not reject rationality in political discourse. However, they do see it as limited and by no means a sufficient condition. There are limits to what can be planned rationally due to the inevitability of unintended consequences. Furthermore, conservatives point to the often bitter consequences of attempts at rational planning, or what might be seen less positively as social engineering. Conservatives are critical of mass social house building and town planning for the same reason (Boyson, 1978; Scruton, 2000).

This critique of rationality and its limitations is most closely associated with Oakeshott and his seminal essay *Rationalism in Politics* (1962). Oakeshott can be seen as an evolutionary conservative. He sees change as inevitable, but where it is necessary it should still be cautious. This is because the consequences of political action are unpredictable: rational planning is prone to failure, if not disaster. Like Kekes, Oakeshott suggests that the purpose of social and civic institutions is to protect our traditional liberties, and these institutions might have to evolve so that these liberties can be preserved. If we are faced with new threats, be they due to globalisation, environmental pollution, demographic change or whatever, those institutions that protect the integrity of a society need to evolve to meet these new threats. Oakeshott is explicit on this evolutionary character, stressing that we develop social institutions out of practice rather than by design and planning. He is fundamentally opposed to rational planning as it demonstrates a misunderstanding of the operation of human experience. His epistemological ideas have a resonance here, not only with the libertarian social philosophy of Hayek (1960, 1988) and Mises (1981), but also the epistemology of Heidegger (1962) and Wittgenstein (1958). Like these other thinkers, Oakeshott's critique is epistemological, in that it calls into question what we can know, and, more importantly, what we need to know for us to be members of a viable polity. One gains knowledge of the world, and progresses through it, by action and not through rationalisation. This scepticism about human knowledge leads Oakeshott to see politics as a practice that is best performed by those experienced in governing.

There is a further strand to Oakeshott's thinking that is important here, and this is his belief in the need to clear the relationship between state and citizen. Like some libertarian thinkers, and particularly Hayek, Oakeshott argued that the role of intermediate institutions such as trade unions, the professions and local government needed to be tightly constrained to ensure that the proper relationship between state and citizen could be fostered and maintained (Devigne, 1994). This point is developed by Scruton (2001) who sees the relationship between state and citizen (or subject, as he would have it according to the British constitutional tradition) as similar to that of parent and child with the consequent reciprocity of fealty, submission and protection that goes with that relationship. It follows from this that institutions that insinuate themselves between the state and citizen are potentially disruptive to this relationship, bringing with them special and particular interests and grievances that might subvert the direct relation between citizens and their protector.

Scruton suggests, along with Oakeshott, that conservatives do not see any purpose in politics other than governing. We indulge in many activities as ends in themselves, and without any larger purpose. We go fishing, read books, watch films and have relationships with others. These activities are not derivative of anything, nor are they subservient. They are sufficient in themselves as ends. Likewise, as Scruton suggests, a society is already an end: 'Its history, institutions and culture are the repositories of human values' (2001,

p. 13). Society is not the means to achieve some future goal, but a worthy end in itself as it is now. Individuals have interests, needs and ends *now*, and there is no reason why these should be sublimated to some future ends that may or may not be realised. Hence Scruton suggests that communism is absurd, as it is at war with the very people it had set out to govern: individuals are prevented from doing what they may wish to do now, in order to prepare 'the people' for some future utopian state in which the ends of others are imposed[3].

For Scruton there are two axiomatic principles of conservative thinking. First, unlike liberalism and socialism, there is no general politics of conservatism, but it is as varied as the forms of social order. Scruton suggests, that for conservatives, there is 'no purpose beyond that of government' (p. 14). He admits that this puts them at a serious disadvantage in relation to socialists: 'they lack any offering with which to stir up the enthusiasm of the crowd. They are concerned solely with the task of government, and their attitude defies translation into a shopping list of social goals' (p. 15). In short, all they can offer is a quiet life. Second, conservatism engages with the surface of things, with the motives, reasons, traditions and values of the society from which it draws its life.

So this sceptical view opposes ends in politics. There are some activities such as friendship and fly-fishing that are pursued for their own ends. These practices depend on skill, and these skills require practice and not the application of book-based theory. We learn how to do many things by practicing them, through emulation and by watching those who are already masters in that skill. But we cannot become proficient by book learning or though classroom instruction. Oakeshott believes that governing is such a skill: it comes through experience and through practice. As Quinton (1993) comments, 'The conservative response to novelty must be a matter of judgement, based on experience, not a business of the application of a set of rigid principles.' (p. 261). One cannot pre-empt political action, merely react to it.

But there is also a second reason for a sceptical approach in politics. Conservatives argue that political ends are almost infinitely contestable, and we cannot agree what the 'correct' ends are. The

---

[3] There is an interesting link here with the libertarianism of Robert Nozick (1974) who argued that it was illegitimate to use one person for the benefit of another. However, the linkage is limited in that Nozick went on to use this principle to suggest that there was no social good, merely individual goods over which no one else had any rights.

ends of individuals and groups are contestable and plural, with no one set necessarily supplanting all others. There is no mechanism to adjudicate between different notions of the good life. It follows therefore that pursuing one end will impact negatively on others and undermine their realisation. We cannot put all our efforts in pursuing one end — be it equality, social justice or choice — without it impacting negatively on others.

Quinton suggests that, beyond the limits of our biology, there is no immutable human nature and therefore there is no necessary set of social and political institutions. Rather, Quinton argues that 'the desirability of such institutions for a conservative is relative to the circumstances of a particular time and place, one in which they are historically established' (1993, p. 247). Political institutions derive from local historical conditions, which cannot, and should not, be transplanted from one culture to another. This represents the Burkean view that 'politics is circumstantial, a matter of expediency, the prudent pursuit of the advantage of a particular community' (Quinton, 1993, p. 251).

Kekes (1998) sees that there may be different traditions, institutions and customs that lead to the good life. There is no single blueprint that is universally applicable and that would inevitably lead to human flourishing. Differing social arrangements have developed within different political and social milieu, and these have a particular instrumentality that might not be transferable to a different situation. Kekes's position, however, is not entirely relativistic. He believes that conservatives will agree that certain attitudes — atomism, for instance — will almost certainly erode any set of traditions and institutions. What he is saying instead is that the desire to conserve will lead to distinct political arrangements and these will depend on particular circumstances. Conservatives see the unplanned and unwritten British constitution as the paradigm case of this distinctiveness (Kirk, 1985; McCue, 1997; Scruton, 2000).

Conservatives have an anti-contractual view of society, in that they believe in non-voluntary duties, allegiances and obligations. Society is not instituted through any social contract, rather human life is definitionally social and therefore there could never have been any state of nature or human existence outside of society. Moreover, the ties that bind one to society are neither optional nor conditional. One has duties that override any individual predisposition.

What goes along with this scepticism about universalism is a pessimism that guards against false hopes and rejects the idea of human perfectibility (Kekes, 1998). Conservatives, being anti-utopians, do not believe that a perfect society is achievable or that evil and misfortune can be eradicated. Conservatives do not believe in progress, or that all situations are improvable. Muller (1997) identifies a belief in human imperfection and what he terms an *epistemological modesty*, in that there are limits to human knowledge. He suggests that conservatives place a dependence on institutions 'with their own rules, norms, restraints and sanctions' (p. 11). These institutions, however, are by no means transferable. Human beings rely on customary rules based on historical experience rather than the continual reinvention of social rules. Like Burke (1999), Muller uses the term 'prejudice' without any pejorative connotation, but as a *pre-judging* of a situation according to our habits, customs and experience. This leads on to further qualities identified by Muller, namely, those of historicism and particularism.

There are three key criticisms of this sceptical view of political institutions. Firstly, it may lead to a degree of fatalism and inertia. If one believes that things are as they are because of traditions, and that there are epistemological limits to what can be planned, then we may be tempted to argue that we should not change at all. If we cannot see into the future, and if we fear the unforeseen, then we may reject all attempts at change. Hence, it might be argued, politics would ossify, and we support an institution merely because of its longevity and what it reminds us of. An example of this is the hereditary principle, which many conservatives still support, but which, we might argue, is not necessary for the proper working of Parliament. But this example — of reforming the House of Lords — offers conservatives a response to this criticism. The Blair government has reduced the number of hereditary peers and signalled its intention to undertake fundamental reform of the Lords. Yet it has no apparent plan, having carried out what it called 'stage one' reforms without any idea of what 'stage two' might consist of. The conservative view would be to argue why it is necessary to change something that works well, in the sense of holding government to account and being a repository of expert opinion which links back to the British political tradition, to replace it with something as yet unknown. Conservatives would want to know why these changes are being made, and whether it is not just a case of change for its own sake, of a governing party desperate to appear 'modern' without any proper conception of what modern means and where it leads to.

A second criticism of this sceptical approach is that support for the status quo is merely a disguise for protecting certain vested interests. Conservatism, it is said, is merely an attempt to preserve traditional institutions and liberties, and seeks to maintain the status quo as a position where one group is dominant. Honderich (1990), for example, argues that the aim of conservative ideology is merely to protect property ownership and existing property relations. Private property rights merely institutionalise existing inequalities. There is thus no particular merit in these institutions if all they do is to entrench property rights that exclude a large number of people. The response to this position is twofold. First, one way of characterising pluralism is as a *series* of vested interests which compete and which may not be reconcilable. The conservative position can be seen to an extent as agonistic, in that the multiplicity of interests within a society cannot always be reconciled. But conservatives such as Kekes (1998) would argue that there are some institutions that are better able to accommodate pluralism than others. Such conservatives would argue that the rule of law and the protection of individual freedoms will best guarantee that no single interest supplants another. Having said this, in UK politics only one party actually identifies itself explicitly with an interest group, and that, of course, is the Labour party.

The second response to the vested interest argument is that it is implausible to suggest that some institutions would have survived, and been maintained in the last century by all parties (including that of organised labour), without their having some utility for all groups. Indeed, it is a matter of fact that all parts of British society have prospered in absolute terms over the last century. What we appear to have, therefore, is a set of institutions in which the party of organised labour can pursue its vested interests without this having overly detrimental effects on other interests.

But perhaps the most serious criticism is that this scepticism towards politics, particularly the Oakeshottian critique of rationality, is that it clashes most with the experience of *really existing conservatism*. In modern politics we can question whether it is possible for a politician to admit that he or she has no real sense of direction and furthermore sees no need for one. Politics is now about the presentation of a vision. Thatcher was not a politician who sat back and awaited events, taking them on their merits (or rather she did not present herself as such). Instead, she had a particular vision of where she wished to take Britain.

But beyond this, there is the belief that politicians have an almost universal competence: there is no longer any area of economic, social and cultural life that is beyond politics. If London is to make a bid to host the Olympic Games, or if we need a new national football stadium, then government has to get involved. Even the millennium celebrations were run by a government minister and consequently directed to meet certain political purposes. There is no real difference between the political parties in this regard: if there is an issue or a problem, politicians are asked to respond and dare not refuse. Current Conservative politicians might say that they want to reduce the role of the state, but this is only at the margins.

Yet we might again ask how much of a contradiction there is here. As we have seen, conservatives rest their politics on a sense of tradition and a particularist view of political culture. Thus if circumstances change—and even if these circumstances might not be as conservatives would have wished—then a conservative, to be consistent, must work within these changes and make the best of them. Pragmatically there is no alternative: if the culture evolves, as we would expect it to, then so must politicians. We might suggest it is precisely the realisation of this essentially conservative idea that has led to the recent electoral successes of the Labour party under Tony Blair[4]. What we need to be aware of is that at different times, and in different situations, one strand of conservative doctrine will tend to dominate over others. It may be that in current conditions, when the Conservative party is in opposition and trying to rebuild after three devastating electoral defeats, the responsive pragmatic approach will dominate.

Organicism

The third doctrine identified by Quinton (1993) is the belief that human beings and society are organically or internally connected. Human beings are not fully independent of the social institutions and practices within which they grow up. We have seen this already when discussing Scruton's Hegelian sense of the conservative instinct. An individual's sense of self depends, in part at least, on his or her appreciation that they are part of a social whole. Moreover, this social whole is specific. They are not part of 'humanity' as such,

---

[4] Blair, we might suggest, is the most convincing conservative politician in Britain since the retirement of Thatcher. Indeed, he might even be more typical of the conservative disposition than Thatcher, who had a rather more developed sense of radicalism than her successor.

nor is it the case that humans need to be part of *any* community. For the conservative what matters is that one feels part of *this* community. As a result of this organic connection it follows that activities of human beings are not susceptible to abstract theorising. We cannot suggest that there is one particular form of social organisation that best fits humanity.

Conservatives again rely on empirical evidence in support of this organicist view. First, they point to the existence of distinct and separate cultures, which are usually defined by a common language. These cultures also have their own sense of community, culture and belonging. Quinton goes so far as to suggest that this is indicative of distinct national characteristics. The second empirical support is that 'Western' political models, such as liberal democracy and Marxism, have not been particularly exportable to the developing world. Where they have been exported they have often been hybridised by the local political culture and have developed into something that is quite specific to that culture[5].

Organicism can be seen as both a logical and metaphysical necessity, as indeed it is in Hegel's *Philosophy of Right* (1991). It is the belief in an absolutely necessary connection to a particular community. However, we need not take such an essentialist position as Hegel. Instead a more down-to-earth position would be simply to suggest that individuals are formed within a particular culture and can do little without a connection into social networks. Nevertheless, this view can still be criticised.

First, it can be suggested that this organicist view neglects the fact that individuals are linked into a multiplicity of social relations ranging from family, school, local community, work group and so on, all of which are likely to be more influential than the state. Individuals may see their primary connection as being to their family or local community rather than to the state. Yet this is only a problem to the organicist view if one ignores the fact that these other social formations are part of the whole and have been formed within it.

The second criticism is that because this position suggests that all parts are linked together, it denies innovation. Now this is undeniably true: there are particular ways of doing things and this means that certain approaches should be seen as inappropriate. But what is important here is that, whilst innovation is denied in politics, *it is not*

---

[5] It might seem ironic that the current example of exporting the 'Western' model, in this case to Afghanistan and Iraq, is being undertaken by neo-conservatives.

in any other sphere. Organicism does not deny innovation in the arts or in science or other aspects of cultural life. This simple form of organic relation is not a metaphysical necessity but a matter of political culture. It is a relation between state and citizen and nothing further.

We are now in a position to take stock. We have discussed three doctrines — traditionalism, scepticism, and organicism — which are central to conservatism. They are clearly connected together and form a unified sense of what conservatism is. However, whilst some important themes have arisen which we shall return to later in our discussion of housing policy, particularly the role of the state and the management of change, there is one theme that needs special consideration. This is because it is central to the conservative disposition, in that it activates the individual within the social whole. But this theme is also important to our discussion of housing policy. This is the notion of ownership.

Owning Things: 'The Essence of Conservatism'

Honderich (1990) suggests that if anything defines conservatism it is property ownership. As a critic of conservatism Honderich wishes to show the negative aspects of property ownership, especially how it manifests a particular vested interest. Indeed, with Thatcherism at least, Honderich seems to believe that the extension of property ownership operated almost as a form of false consciousness, lulling working-class property owners into the mistaken belief that they now had a stake in the system. Honderich, I would suggest, is essentially correct, even though his aim is to disparage these ideas of ownership and social stability. Whether we see these ideas as negative is, of course, another matter. What we need to do, therefore, is first consider the conservative justification of property ownership and then we may consider whether Honderich's criticisms have any validity.

What is interesting is that, when the discussion turns to property ownership, conservative thinkers seem most able to articulate a theoretical position. It is as if, in discussing ownership, they can place conservatism on firmer foundations, something, as it were, more solid on which to base a justification for the conservative disposition. Hence Scruton (2001) becomes more categorical when discussing property, or what he describes as 'the absolute and ineradicable need for private property' (p. 92). We can again see a Hegelian strain in his thinking when he states:

> Ownership is the primary relation through which man and nature come together. It is therefore the first stage in the socialising of objects, and the condition of all higher institutions. It is not necessarily a product of greed or exploitation, but it is necessarily a part of the process whereby people free themselves from the power of things, transforming resistant nature into compliant image. Through property man imbues his world with will, and begins therein to discover himself as a social being. (p. 92)

Without property we cannot identify any object in the world as our own, and hence we have no right to use any object, nor can we expect others to allow us access to it (not that they could, of course, because they too would have no rights over it either). Without rights of ownership everything is merely an object of desire. Objects without ownership can play no part in social relations: there can be no exchange, no gifts, and no transfers from one person to another.

Scruton argues that, if people are to become fully aware of themselves as agents who are capable of independent action within a social whole, then they need to see the world in terms of rights, responsibility and freedom. He suggests that it is 'The institution of property [that] allows them to do this' (p. 93). By making an object mine I can now use it for my purposes. I am able to be more active because my possibilities have been increased. But I am also given a responsibility, for I now have to determine how it can be used, whether I should share my access, and so on. As Scruton states 'Through property an object ceases to be a mere inanimate thing, and becomes instead the focus of rights and obligations' (p. 93). Through property ownership 'the object is lifted out of mere 'thinghood' and rendered up to humanity' (p. 93) It bears the imprint of social relations and reflects back to the owner 'a picture of himself as a social being' (p. 93), as someone now with the capability of relations with others. Property ownership is therefore seen by Scruton as a primary social relation. It is what allows us access into the social world, as beings able to achieve our ends.

Having given this rather abstract justification of property ownership Scruton then identifies the main form of property we experience. Ownership, as it were, grounds the self into the social world. As he states, instead of being at loose in the world, an individual is 'at home' (p. 93). He goes on:-

> It is for this reason that a person's principal proprietary attitude is towards his immediate surroundings—house, room, furniture—towards those things with which he is, so to speak, min-

gled. It is the home, therefore, that is the principal sphere of property, and the principal locus of the gift. (p. 93)

The most important form of property is the home, as this is the primary relation. It is what we live within and what therefore becomes part of us. When we own those things around us — the house and its contents — we are better able to control our surroundings and disburse our personal and social obligations. The family unit is where we show responsibility to others, where our primary obligations are held and where we are most able to express our generosity.

This suggests that Scruton sees no necessary connection between possession and consumption. Indeed he tries expressly to disconnect the two concepts. He correctly states that consumption does not presuppose ownership, and would take place even in a state of nature or communist paradise: comrades still need to eat. Consumption can be seen as individual, as something that relates to individuals' needs and desires. What it does not show is the social essence of property, and accordingly these should be seen as distinct notions. What ownership does offer is stability: 'The important aspect of property is its stable aspect, in which ownership is conceived as permanent or semi-permanent. For the full fruition of the sense of property there must be permanent objects of possession' (Scruton, 2001, p. 94).

The linkage between ownership on the one hand, and home and household on the other, is clearly important then to conservatives. Home is where private property becomes something shared. It is where things are simply *ours*. Scruton states that 'It is for this reason that conservatives have seen the family and private property as institutions which stand or fall together. The family has its life in the home, and the home demands property for its establishment' (p. 94). Importantly, this is not merely some historical accident, or just, as Marxists would have it, the model of the bourgeois family imposed on society as a whole. As Scruton is keen to ask, where and when, outside socialist and utopian futurist fictions, has there been the non-bourgeois family? Accordingly, he argues that property rights are as important to working-class families in council housing as they are to the middle classes. Property is a particular form of right and hence 'the occupancy of a council flat is a property right ... it enables the proletarian family to accumulate goods and gadgetry ... in a manner which changes the aspect of the home' (p. 95). Council housing is determined by property relations, and the rights and obligations involved offer possibilities which convert space into a home.

This position is supported by Quinton (1993) who stresses the importance of property as a means of stabilising societies. Likewise, he too links ownership to the family, in that property allows family members to look after themselves. He also concurs with Scruton by suggesting that conservatives believe there is no plausible alternative to the family.

But this is, of course, a position that can be criticised, both in the abstract and because of the effects of policies such as the Right to Buy, which can be seen as being based on this idea of property. I wish here to restrict the criticisms to the more abstract argument, relying particularly on Honderich's critique. His view is important in that he takes what could be called the 'standard' critique of rights, that differentiates between freedom and capability. We need to distinguish between those who have the resources as well as the freedom to act, and those who merely have the latter. In consequence, Honderich argues that property ownership merely favours one particular class. He states that 'the conservative society ... enlarges the total of what is distributed according to the ability to pay and decreases the total of what is distributed according to need' (1989, p. 89). He sees property ownership as a zero sum game, where allowing the few to gain more deprives the majority from realising their desires. He suggests that 'the conservative desire and strategy to increase to a limited extent the number of holders of some small amount of property, notably a home or a few shares' does not carry 'the great benefits of other amounts and forms of property (p. 93) . Owner occupation does not, Honderich seems to believe, allow these individuals to accumulate capital, and they are therefore not part of the property-owning class in the classical Marxist sense.

This is, of course, a fairly traditional argument used by opponents of home ownership. They seek to differentiate between different types of ownership and thus to suggest that home owners are in some way being deluded. This view has been justifiably criticised by libertarian and anarchist writers such as Turner (1976) and Ward (1985). What it neglects is the significance of what Honderich rather patronisingly refers to as a 'small amount of property' to the individuals themselves. The importance of property is not related to consumption or to accumulation, but to what it allows individuals to do. As we shall see when we discuss the Right to Buy in chapter four, the importance of extending home ownership is that it extends a personal relation into a socially significant one. Property ownership offers the most effective means for institutionalising privacy: it protects private relations and does this through the socialisation of key relations.

But this does not answer Honderich's criticism of the exclusive nature of ownership, whereby the holdings of a minority deprive access to it by the majority. But when we start to consider what it is that Conservative governments did in Britain in the late twentieth century, we see that they have actually attempted to do the opposite. Their policies towards owner occupation have not been about exclusion but about distribution, with extending ownership further. As Scruton (2001) has suggested:

> ... the essential connection between household and family is undeniable. It follows that conservatives must be concerned with the distribution of property, and not only its accumulation. Given their belief in the political importance of the family, and their reliance on family loyalties in forming respect towards an established political order, they must desire the distribution of property through all classes of society, in accordance with whatever conception of household might be generic to each of them. (p. 95)

What concerns conservatives is the extension of ownership, and this, as we shall see is a major theme in contemporary housing policy. Indeed, we might even say, regardless of any changes in governments since 1997, it still remains the central priority of housing policy.

Some Emerging Themes

This has been a necessarily brief discussion of conservatism. It has concentrated only on the British (or even English) variety and hence emphasised certain aspects and ignored others that are more significant in American or European conservatism (for example, faith in USA, and corporatism in France and Germany)[6]. However, I believe it does allow us to draw out a number of themes that we can take forward to our discussion on housing policy.

The first theme is a belief in government for its own sake, which leads to a pragmatic or managerial approach. To an extent this pre-empts some of the discussion in chapters two and three, but it is already eminently clear that an emphasis on processes and plural-

---

[6] An increasingly significant form I have largely neglected is neo-conservatism. This is because it does not really exist much outside the USA, and there is little evidence of it in UK politics. However, as I discuss briefly in chapter six, there is some reason to see Blair as a neo-conservative.

ism will be unlikely to achieve specific outcomes at any cost. The second theme is that conservatives are consistently critical of government planning and their desire to enhance individual rather than state activity; and the third is the considerable emphasis they place on property ownership. These last themes are interesting in a further way, in that they link conservatism, with all its stressing of traditions, scepticism, and resistance to change, with that other ideology that is frequently linked to the Thatcher period in particular, namely, libertarianism. This ideology is based on a deep distrust of government and 'collective' approaches to politics, and the sanctity of private property ownership. We therefore need to consider libertarianism in some detail and assess what impact it might be said to have had on Conservative thought and policy making.

Chapter Two

The Influence of Libertarianism

Not Just a Disposition

If there is some doubt as to whether conservatism is an ideology, there is no doubt when it comes to libertarianism. Libertarianism is much more typical of political ideologies in that it proposes a set of core principles and seeks to develop political programmes that would implement them. There is no attempt to hide behind apparently obfuscatory notions such as 'attitude' and 'disposition' to mask one's embarrassment at actually stating anything as positive as a programme of political action.

What is more at issue is the label that one chooses to give to this political programme. If we were to look for the historical foundations of libertarianism we would go back to such luminaries as Mandeville, Smith, Mill and Spencer, all of whom have been and are referred to as liberals. Indeed some libertarians suggest that they are merely carrying on this great liberal tradition centred on the efficacy of markets, spontaneous social action and individual liberty (Hayek, 1978, 1988). However, as Seldon (2005) has stated, the term 'liberal' now has a particular baggage as a result of the historical impact of the British Liberal party, which since the end of the nineteenth century has been more concerned with state provision than individual freedom, and in the 2005 General Election was the only major party to call for an increase in taxation. In addition, over the last thirty years the term has been appropriated by the left in America to denote those who are in favour of permissive social policies and state support to redistribute resources to those on low income: in the USA to be a liberal is therefore the opposite of being a conservative. Hence, in both Britain and the USA the term 'liberal' now carries with it a distinctly different strain from that of a century or more ago. Liberals are in favour of state action rather than against it, and support tempering the effects of markets rather than freeing them up from regulation and government intervention. So for thinkers like Seldon (2005) one cannot be happy to apply the term liberal. Seldon and other thinkers such as Conway (1995) have chosen to refer to themselves as classical liberals to demonstrate their affinity with Smith and Mill, and to distinguish themselves from the statism of modern liberals. Hayek, in his essay *Why I am Not a Conservative* (1960), chooses to define himself as a Whig, again with the intention of directly associating himself with the liberalism of Mandeville and Smith in the seventeenth and eighteenth centuries.

There is a reluctance on the part of these thinkers to describe themselves as libertarian. Partly this is because it was seen, by Hayek at least, as a rather ugly neologism, when his expressed aim was to connect with a set of principles he could trace back three centuries. Hayek, Seldon and others have been keen to stress that they are not inventing a new set of doctrines or philosophy, but are rediscovering ideas that once dominated before state intervention and socialism. As a result they see it as important to embed their ideas in time — to see it as a 'classical' philosophy rather than a modern one. Thinkers in the USA, however, have fewer scruples in using a newer term, and in any case would tend to find the term 'liberal' to be too sullied by its appropriation by the American left. The use of 'liberal' to denote the left is now so pervasive — it can almost be a cipher for 'socialist' — that those on the right seeking to promote liberty and private property need an alternative.

I would suggest that libertarianism has now joined the mainstream as a term for a set of principles, doctrines and policies, so that we can use it and expect some general understanding of its meaning. Indeed if one were to ask a reasonably educated person to name a libertarian it is likely they would first make reference to Hayek. It is therefore a term I wish to use instead of liberal, so as to ensure there is no ambiguity regarding my meaning.

I ended chapter one by stressing three themes that characterised conservatism, stating that two of them in particular could be related to libertarianism. Indeed one could suggest that these two can almost be said to define libertarianism. If this is indeed the case, then, we already have a ready link between conservative and libertarian ideas. These two themes are, first, a general scepticism and critical attitude towards government activity with a preference towards enhancing individual choice and decision making, and, second, a support for private property ownership. As we shall see, these are clearly fundamental tenets of belief also for libertarians. However, it is necessary to state that the justifications for these principles might differ from those of conservatives. But before hastening to any conclusions that link conservatism and libertarianism, we need to hold in mind that there were three principles and that conservatives might not grant them all equal importance. Indeed it might be that the theme that we have not tried to link — the desire for gradualism and pragmatism — would be seen by conservatives as the most important, so that it overrides the other two. Indeed, without entirely pre-empting the discussion on libertarianism, this is indeed what I wish to suggest and thus want to insist that the conservative strain dominates over the libertarian. However, there is some work needed before this claim can be left to stand, and so first I shall try to define what libertarianism is.

Defining Libertarianism

Whilst it is relatively easy to state what libertarianism is, this should not be taken to mean that there is no dispute between libertarians, or that all arrive at the same conclusions regarding policy. Moreover, different theorists arrive at their libertarianism from different routes, for example Narveson (1988) uses contract theory, whilst Rasmussen and Den Uyl (1991) rely on an Aristotelian justification; Hayek (1960) can be seen as a consequentialist in the style of Mill, whilst Nozick (1974) is a deontologist in the tradition of Kant. These distinctions also point us to the more overtly theoretical nature of libertarianism compared to the thinking of conservatives, who despite the Hegelian sophistications of Scruton (2001), tend to be rather more grounded in common sense and human nature than high theory.

But despite these differences between theorists, we can offer a rather straightforward definition of libertarianism with which I believe all of the above would concur. Boaz (1997) in his introduction to a libertarian reader including thinkers ranging from the ancient Chinese poet Lao-Tzu to the contemporary American economist Milton Friedman, suggests a number of central ideas that characterise libertarian thought, and which tend to be linked together. First, he sees a scepticism about political power and its effects; second, he points to the importance of the dignity of the individual to these writers, and this is linked to the third characteristic of a deep respect for individual rights; fourth, Boaz points to the importance of spontaneity as an ordering principle in society, so that societies are not created by design but develop out of the actions of human beings relating to each other; and finally, he states the importance of peace as a principle that libertarians hold dear, seeing the power held by the state as a major cause of conflict within and between nations. These are rather broad characteristics and it may well be that some thinkers emphasise one to the exclusion of others.

However, I believe it is possible to simplify or reduce these five characteristics into a simpler formula on which they all rest. If we ask why we should be sceptical of political power, why we stress spontaneity and why we seek peace, we are likely to respond that this is because of the centrality of individual dignity and individual rights to any notion of the political. Libertarians tend to see the state as pernicious because it does things which individuals can and should do for themselves, and might do better than the state as they have a more intimate knowledge of their needs than any bureaucracy could manage. The state also does things to and against individuals, such as conscripting them to fight wars and confiscating part of their income to pay for it. Likewise a spontaneous social order can only be derived from a situation where individuals are free to interact without being overly circumscribed by existing institutions; and war is the most extreme denigration of individuals, with them turned into mere cogs in the military machine serving a state rather than their kith and kin.

This means that we can define libertarianism as 'the belief that individual liberty is the most important entity there is' (King, 2000, p. 49). Perhaps the most famous recent formulation of this is the opening sentence of Nozick's *Anarchy, State and Utopia* (1974): 'Individuals have rights and there are things no person or group may do to them (without violating their rights)' (p. ix). Nozick has been criticised for not explaining *why* individuals have rights (Wolff, 1991), but this was not really his purpose. Rather he wished to use this assertion of principle as a starting point to consider what form of state could be justified so that this position on individual rights could be maintained. What is important about Nozick's position is that he begins with a rejection of atomism, seeing libertarianism as being instead about social relations. He is concerned not with what individuals do with their rights (or, indeed, where these rights have come from), but how they can be protected, and he realises that this depends upon the actions of others: my rights are only secure if others refrain from doing certain things like invading my house, stealing my money and goods, harassing me, and so on. Just as we found that conservatism was based on social relations, with individual freedom being derived from a sense of order, so does libertarianism, at least of the Nozickean variety.

Central to Nozick's argument is the side-constraint on the behaviour of all individuals to ensure that individual rights are not infringed. Nozick does not particularly consider the extent of this side-constraint, but a moment's thought will indicate that this is indeed quite a restriction. As he himself states with a vivid example — 'I can put my knife where I like but not in your chest' — the existence of side-constraints places considerable limits on individual behaviour, and would entail a detailed and highly developed legal code to uphold rights. But what is essential to Nozick's argument, as with most libertarians, is that the state should only do those things it is necessary for it to do and that cannot be done by anyone else. This is what Nozick referred to as the ultraminimal or 'night-watchman' state.

Of course, we can question just how influential Nozick has been in the UK (or even in the USA for that matter). Nozick is commonly seen as the thinker who helped to alter the intellectual climate and therefore to make libertarian and capitalist ideas intellectually respectable again. Prior to *Anarchy, State and Utopia*, there was not an intellectually credible argument for the libertarian or classical liberal position by a modern writer, and so he is important for that reason alone. However, his work might be seen as rather too rigorous for practical politics, and indeed has little in the manner of direct political prescription. Where Nozick is relevant to our discussion here is that he presents a libertarian argument remarkable for its consistency, so that we are able to grasp what the full import of libertarianism might be. Nozick, was himself critical of the 'pick'n'mix' attitude of politicians who were prepared to accept his prescriptions for the economy, but not his arguments for the abolition of immigration controls or against any restrictions on the sexual behaviour of consenting adults. So Nozick offers us a clear picture of libertarianism, as well as presenting us with some of the difficulties that politicians have to contend with if they are to implement such a set of principles.

Nozick's starting point, as have seen, is the inviolability of individual rights. Individuals have self-ownership and they should not therefore be constrained by any agency or being unless their actions are violating the rights of others. This position leads Nozick to assert that there is no notion of the public or social good, merely benefits and costs that might accrue to individuals. The actions of the state have the effect of benefiting some individuals by adding to their property, but this is arrived at through forcibly removing the property of others. Hence he states:

> there is no *social entity* with a good that undergoes some sacrifice for its own good. There are only individual people, different individual people, with their own individual lives. Using one of these people for the benefit of others, uses him and benefits the others. Nothing more. What happens is that something is done to him for the sake of others. Talk of an overall social good covers this up. (Intentionally?) To use a person in this way does not sufficiently respect and take account of the fact that he is a separate person, that his is the only life he has. *He* does not get some over-balancing good from his sacrifice, and no one is entitled to force this upon him - least of all a state or government that claims his allegiance (as other individuals do not) and that therefore scrupulously must be *neutral* between its citizens. (pp. 32–3, author's emphasis)

What Nozick relies on here is the second formulation of Kant's Categorical Imperative which states that one should act in such a way as to see another human being always as an end in themselves and never simply as a means (Kant, 1997). According to Nozick's reading of Kant, this means that it is illegitimate to use one person for the benefit of another. What makes this argument distinctive is the assertion that there is no such entity as the social good. One cannot calculate some utilitarian end state whereby society as a whole is better off because we have used the property of one for the benefit of another: we cannot sacrifice someone for a supposed greater good.

This is perhaps a more rigorous way of stating that the government has no money of its own to spend, merely that of its citizens. Accordingly Nozick can state:

> There is no *central* distribution, no person or group entitled to control all the resources, jointly deciding how they are to be doled out. What each person gets, he gets from others who give to him in exchange for something, or as a gift. In a free society, diverse persons control different resources, and new holdings arise out of the voluntary exchanges and actions of persons ... The total result is the product of many individual decisions which the different individuals are entitled to make. (1974, pp. 149–50)

From this starting point Nozick develops the idea of a just distribution based on entitlement to property (or, as he terms it, holdings). This consists of three principles. The first principle derives from the *original acquisition of holdings*, or 'the appropriation of unheld things'

(p. 150). Thus, 'A person who acquires a holding in accordance with the principle of justice in acquisition is entitled to that holding' (p. 151)

Secondly, which in practice would be the main form, there is the *transfer of holdings*, which deals with voluntary exchanges and gifts. Thus, 'A person who acquires a holding in accordance with the principle of justice in transfer, from someone else entitled to the holding, is entitled to the holding' (p. 151). No one is entitled to a holding, according to Nozick except by repeated applications of these two principles.

However, some holdings have derived from fraud, enslavement or other illegitimate action. There is therefore the need for a third principle, which Nozick refers to as 'the rectification of injustice in holdings' (p. 152). This concerns dealing with the question: 'If past injustice has shaped present holdings in various ways, some identifiable, some not, what now, if anything, ought to be done to rectify these injustices?' (p. 152).

These three principles determine whether an individual's holdings are just and 'If each person's holdings are just, the total set (distribution) of holdings is just' (p. 153). In some ways Nozick is offering a typical libertarian position, which sees that the matter of distribution is determined by production (Barry, 1986). Thus if one has legitimate ownership of property, the issue of its distribution is settled.

There are only two exceptions to this. Firstly, as we have seen, one's rights are constrained to the extent that one does not coerce others. We have already suggested that this would be a major limitation on individual action, and one that would make any resulting Nozickean society much more similar to current western democracies than many of his critics (and perhaps Nozick himself) would admit. The second exception Nozick makes is the need for a night-watchman state to enforce contracts between individuals, so that our rights might be safeguarded.

According to Nozick, a key distinction between his theory of justice and others is that not only is his theory historical, but it also refrains from specifying a particular pattern or end result. In this way, he connects up justice and individual freedom. A patterned principle is one that prescribes the form of distribution or prejudges outcomes within a society. Thus it is seeing a particular distribution (an end result) as just. However, for Nozick, this situation *cannot* be just, as it involves the continual interference with individual liberty to maintain this pattern of distribution. It is here that Nozick uses his famous 'Wilt Chamberlain' example. This is a thought experiment where he imagines a community where income equality is established. Throughout a season many individuals choose to pay a voluntary premium to watch a particularly talented basketball player (Chamberlain), which is paid to the player. At the end of the year the basketball player is much wealthier than anyone else in that community. But this has arisen entirely from voluntary acts, and without any coercion. Nozick questions on what basis it is acceptable to return to strict equality, a situation that could only be arrived at by considerable and continual intervention, when this inequality has derived entirely from voluntary acts. The point that Nozick makes is that equality can only be arrived at by massive and continuous state action. But more importantly, he shows that inequality not only can but will derive from the actions of free individuals doing voluntary acts, any of which can be justified on its own terms, be it choosing to work harder or to pay to watch basketball.

Nozick's work is both complex and wide-ranging, and this discussion has only given a flavour of it. My aim has not been to suggest that it has influenced policy makers greatly, but rather to show many of the crucial libertarian arguments and their implications with the greatest economy. Indeed, it is here that the very purity of his position is of most use to us. Nozick's position shows the effect of an emphasis on individual rights and the effect they would have on the size and nature of state action and the role of voluntary action through markets. We can now progress to some rather more grounded and therefore more influential figures in terms of practical politics, which, after all, is the ground which Conservatives wish to see themselves staking out.

Hayek

Perhaps the most influential libertarian thinker on British politics is Hayek. He was frequently referred to as Mrs Thatcher's favourite thinker and there are stories of her insisting that ministers and civil servants read his *The Constitution of Liberty* (1960) (Ebenstein, 2001). Whether this has any truth to it, and indeed whether the former prime minister was ever really familiar with the work herself is open to debate. As Ebenstein (2001) reports, Hayek kept his distance from the Thatcherites in the 1980s even as he relished the higher profile it gave to him and to his ideas.

A Conservative Consensus? 55

Hayek, like Nozick, puts great stress on individual action. However, his starting point is not Kantian deontology, but the belief that markets and individual decision making are quite simply the most efficient means of creating wealth and a sustainable social order. Like classical liberals in the seventeenth and eighteenth centuries, Hayek argued that the great virtue of market systems was their spontaneity and the results of this. Hayek referred to the market process as a catallaxy (Hayek, 1982). By this he meant to convey the sense that markets are not confined to a specific place and cannot be controlled by regulation. Rather he spoke of 'the cosmos of a market' (1982, II, p. 108), as something that cannot be governed by one end. Instead 'it serves the multiplicity of separate and incommensurable ends of all its separate members' (1982, II, p. 108), and being made up of the incommensurable it is unpredictable and endlessly creative. A catallaxy is therefore 'the special kind of spontaneous order produced by the market through people acting within the rules of the law of property, tort and contract' (p. 109).

This sense of spontaneity can be seen as a form of invisible hand argument. This notion is commonly seen as deriving from Smith (1976a, 1976b), but it can also be found in various forms in Ferguson (1966), Hume (1978), and from seventy five years before Smith, in Mandeville's *Fable of the Bees* (1988). An invisible hand explanation can be defined as identifying 'any argument that proposes to show how some regular phenomenon emerged or could have emerged 'spontaneously' or 'unintendedly' from the actions of many persons' (Koppl, 1994, p.192). It is where many individuals (and institutions) following their own interests arrive at an outcome which none of them would have intended. It is the emergence of a pattern that is not predicted by any of the individual players when deciding what actions best suit their purposes. Nozick too makes use of this form of explanation, which he terms a 'fundamental explanation' (1974, p. 6) and sees it as being the most satisfying form of explanation. This is because it purports to explain a situation using none of the variable from within that situation, so a particular political realm will be explained using none of the elements of that realm and can thus be said to be a non-political explanation. As the explanation comes from outside the realm it can be presented as a total explanation.

What we see therefore is a pattern in libertarian thought that emphasises the spontaneous and unintended as key mechanisms for both social action and our understanding of it. What is interesting is that when Hayek develops this in the political we can see similarities with the ideas of conservatives, and in particular the idea of evolution we saw in Oakeshott's *Rationalism in Politics* (1962).

Hayek, in what is a similar if more general discussion than Oakeshott's, makes the distinction between two types of rationalism, which he calls *constructivist* and *evolutionary*. Constructivist rationalists believe that all human institutions and behaviour are the result of human reason and will. Human beings can therefore master society and come to control and reform it. It is therefore the belief that human institutions can be constructed to achieve particular desired aims. Hayek contrasts this with evolutionary rationalism, which is an attempt to understand how civilisation has developed, but with the attendant recognition of the limits of our current knowledge, and thus the likelihood of unintended and unforeseen consequences. In a sense this perspective is one which distrusts human reason and eschews the grand design. According to Hayek, evolutionary rationalism is embodied in the ideas of Burke (1999), Hume (1978), Mandeville (1988) and Smith (1976a, 1976b). It assumes that knowledge accumulates through individual action and experience, but in an unpredictable way, and therefore without any preformed plan. Indeed even where there is a plan this will quickly go awry as the accumulated decisions of millions of players, all acting according to their own interests, begin to impact on the plan. This implies that social change is better seen as a slow development caused by this untold number of actions, and rather than resulting from deliberative acts of manipulation. This idea of evolution is clearly linked to Hayek's discussion of catallaxy, with its sense of a cosmos of actions all swirling in an apparently uncoordinated mass, but which seems to arrive at beneficial outcomes for its players.

This advocacy of evolution and the rejection of constructivist rationality led Hayek to oppose the centralising and aggregating tendencies of modern social policy. He suggests that the key problem here is the idea that society has needs and requirements over and above the constituent parts of that society. Hayek suggests notions such as the 'national economy' and 'the needs of society' are fallacious and indeed dangerous, in that they lead to the belief that it is some agency's responsibility to manage and control distribution within a society (Shand, 1990). Rather we should see social entities as abstractions which can be reduced to the actions of individuals (Scott, 1995; Shand, 1990). A particular target for Hayek was the concept of social justice, which he saw as a mirage (Hayek, 1982). Social justice is based on a fallacious coupling of what ought to be two distinct entities: justice and the idea of the social. Hayek argues that social justice is an abuse of the word 'justice' which 'threatens to destroy the conception of law which made it the safeguard of individual freedom' (1982, vol. 2, p. 62). The problem with the term 'social' is that it encourages the 'substitution for individual morality of artificial values of a centrally controlled society and the presumption that 'society' has real aims superior to those of individuals' (Shand, 1990, p. 124).

According to Hayek, a proper use of the concept of justice would be one of rules which could generally be applied equally to all citizens. For Hayek, justice can only relate to the treatment accorded to individuals, and therefore an enforced distribution — one done without the express consent of those footing the bill — is by definition unjust, as it treats individuals differently. Hayek sees that this may lead to outcomes which are unequal or unfair, but that these outcomes are not unjust if they have derived from rules which affect everyone equally. What Hayek is adamant about, however, is that a society based on spontaneous action and these rules of justice will be the most affluent and free that it is possible to arrive at.

Hayek's libertarianism would allow for a higher level of state involvement than that of Nozick. Indeed it is quite possible to see Hayek's model of the catallaxy and justice as compatible with authoritarian government (Haworth, 1994) in a way that it is not possible to associate with Nozick. However, this was by no means Hayek's intention. What he is keen to stress is the primacy of markets as the mechanism for day-to-day decision making rather than overt political processes. In this sense, he is similar to a number of other thinkers who come under the general heading of libertarian or classical liberal.

Friedman

Perhaps the most high profile libertarian intellectual in the 1980s was the American economist Milton Friedman. Along with his Chicago School colleagues, he was critical of Keynesian demand management and the effects it had had on Western economies. Accordingly, he called for a return to supply-side economics, micro-economic analysis and the control of inflation. His influence over governments in the 1980s and beyond was through his espousal of monetarism and the belief that inflation was the key problem to be tackled by government economic management (Green, 1987).

However, Friedman by no means restricted himself to economics, but extended his thought to social policy and the role of the state. In the book he wrote with his wife, *Free to Choose* (1980), he argued that economic freedom was necessary for civil liberty, and therefore a key problem was the manner in which the modern state sought to control the economy and thus hamper the ability of individuals to take decisions for themselves. He saw the problem deriving from an overvaluation of equality as a political aim. This, he felt, has led to an accretion of power in the hands of the state to try to ensure that all citizens have their share and that wealth is redistributed accordingly. However, Friedman argued that this emphasis on equality of outcomes stifles initiative and wealth creation, in that individuals cannot gain the full benefit from their hard work and risk taking. Like nearly all libertarians, Friedman sees that state bureaucracies place too much emphasis on distribution and not on production: they see the issue of production as being settled and therefore the state should be concerned primarily with who gets what.

Friedman became particularly associated with two particular policies which he argued would radically enhance choice and independence, as well as extend market disciplines into public services. First, he argued for education vouchers as a key reform in the public sector, giving parents the choice of which school to send their children to, and cutting out bureaucracy. This was a policy that found favour with other classical liberals such as Seldon (1977) in the UK and was also espoused by public choice theorists. The argument was that governments fail to deliver efficient and effective services such as schools due to the impact and influence of special interests, which are encouraged by bargaining over political power. Professionals and trade unions, as well as politicians and bureaucrats have particular interests which do not necessarily match or even approximate to the interests of the consumers of these public services. What we see here is another link with conservatism, which stressed the impact that intermediate institutions can have on the relationship between state and citizen (in the role of consumer here). The second policy Friedman championed was the shift to cash-based welfare supports instead of subsidies to public and private agencies. Individuals should be given the cash directly and be able to make their own choices in terms of pension provision, health care and housing. Friedman argued that these cash supports be integrated with the tax system, with the development of negative income tax for the poor (Green, 1987). The principle behind this proposal was that individuals are better at making the choices that affect them than bureaucrats and agencies, which will have their own interests to further.

Like Hayek, Friedman wishes to assert the primacy of markets as an alternative and more effective means of co-ordinating economic activity. Markets are the principal manner in which choice can be expressed. In particular, Friedman emphasised the centrality of the price mechanism, which, he argued, allows for co-ordination without coercion. Price, for Friedman has three functions: first, to transmit information about consumer behaviour; second, to provide incentives to limit or reduce costs; and third, to determine who gets what, i.e., the distribution of income. He argued that the price mechanism can be seen as a form of continuous democracy in which individuals' wants and needs are responded to directly. Like Seldon (2005) and other classical liberals, he places consumer sovereignty in markets above democracy as a means of directly achieving one's wants and needs.

Public Choice

We have seen in Friedman a strand of libertarianism that suggests that government cannot be trusted. This is based on the premise that government is not neutral. This insight has been developed most fully by public choice theorists such as Buchanan (1986), Niskanen (1973) and Tulloch (1976). These thinkers have argued that political parties are like entrepreneurs, but they seek to maximise their vote instead of their income. Government in this sense acts like a market, with each player following his or her own interests and seeking to achieve their private ends. This is what Tulloch (1979) defined as the vote motive. As Green (1987) states, 'Political parties, therefore, become vote-seeking coalitions which respond to pressure groups by a process of vote-buying at the common expense' (p. 100).

It is interesting in this regard that Seldon (2005) chooses the term the *economics of politics* as a better and more accurate description of this school of thought than public choice. This is because, as Green (1987) has argued, 'The chief insight of the public choice school is that there is no escape from private motivations'. He goes on: 'however the state presents itself, and however pervasive it becomes, the struggle for private advancement continues in other guises' (p. 107). What public choice does therefore is to suggest that the same motivations we see in a market, of maximisation and self interest, are equally in the political process.

However, as Niskanen has argued, there is no motivation for bureaucrats in their normal situation to be efficient. They face none of the pressures of a market and are thus able to benefit from this protected position. The answer, as critics such as Seldon (2005) have stated, is to instigate market disciplines into the public sector to create incentives for greater efficiency. The most effective incentive, it is argued, is to mirror the market itself and institute direct competition between providers.

The Influence of Libertarianism

I suggested at the beginning of this chapter that libertarianism shared with conservatism a scepticism towards government and the support for private property. We can therefore see a ready connection between the two ideologies. But this, of course, does not mean that they are one and the same. There are some important differences in emphasis and in style, particularly the sense of libertarianism being much more purposive than conservatism.

Perhaps the one area that libertarians stress more strongly is that of markets. Hayek, Friedman and the public choice school clearly place markets and the price mechanism as the key elements in the political process, going so far as to see the market as more expressive of the needs and wants of individuals than democracy is (Seldon, 2005). However, conservatives are rather more cautious in their support of markets. Scruton (2001) for example, has stated that there is no inevitable or necessary link between capitalism and conservatism. His view is that where capitalism helps to meet the ends of the conservative it should be used, but it always needs to be controlled. Many British conservatives of Scruton's type, centred around the journal *The Salisbury Review* are critical of global capitalism for its denigration of the local and the particular, and see nothing but adventurism and economic imperialism in the American and British 'war on terror' that led to the invasions of Afghanistan and Iraq. For these conservatives, globalisation and the influence of American culture and commerce are as much of a threat as they are for the counter-cultural 'no logo' left.

Accordingly, for some traditional conservatives there was rather too much market and not enough state for their own liking. For these sorts of conservatives there is no automatic connection between conservatism and capitalism. Conservatism predates capitalism: in Britain, the Tory party has historically been the party of the country, of landed interests, rather than of *laissez faire* and free markets. The notion of a radical reforming government — of the Thatcher revolution — was something to be viewed with horror: just what was happening to the party of Church and nation?

Many conservatives therefore would not concur with the outright anti-statism of libertarianism. Whilst they might agree that the state needs to shrink, conservatives, including Thatcher, argued that this could only be achieved by a strong central state that could force changes on intermediate institutions and local government (Gamble, 1988).

As a result libertarians and classical liberals such as Seldon (2005) have been critical of the Thatcher government for not going far enough, even as they have welcomed much of the government's achievements. Whilst he supported the privatisation of public utilities, Seldon has been critical of the Conservatives for not extending their privatisation programme into the public sector. He is critical of the rejection of education vouchers, and of the failure to tackle the monolithic bureaucracy of the National Health Service. In short, libertarians felt that the state did not shrink anything like as much as it should.

But having said this, Seldon sees the Thatcher governments as being immensely significant, especially for breaching the citadel of collectivism and showing that ideas based on individual liberty, capitalistic wealth creation and markets could work to enhance both affluence and personal freedom. He was also prescient enough to comment that the Thatcher 'revolution' made it impossible for an unreformed Labour party ever to rule again. Only after major reforms of its aims and structures could Labour ever hope to regain power (Seldon, 2005). The point here, which is particularly relevant to our study, is that the only way the Labour party could regain power was by remodelling itself in the light of the fundamental shift brought about by the Thatcher years. So even if libertarians find fault with the actions of the Conservative governments between 1979 and 1997, they still see much to praise and support.

So, in the light of these comments, just what influence did libertarianism have on Conservatism and how compatible was it with conservatism as a dispositional ideology? Devigne (1994) shows that there were similarities between Oakeshott and Hayek,[1] particularly in terms of seeking to limit intermediate institutions and the role of the state to allow for greater civil association. We have also shown

---

[1] Hayek (1899–1992) and Oakeshott (1901–90) were almost exact contemporaries.

that there is some concurrence at the epistemological level, particularly relating to the evolutionary nature of social change and the importance of spontaneity and the unintended. There is a common critique of the ability of a central rational authority to plan the complex needs of a community that runs through both libertarian and conservative thought. Indeed, Hayek's discussion of an evolutionary rationality has led to some critics to see him as a conservative rather than a liberal or libertarian, something he was adamant in denying (Hayek, 1960).

Whilst it was the case that Hayek and Friedman both had significantly higher public profiles than Oakeshott or any other conservative thinker, hindsight suggests that their actual impact was less than one might initially suggest. Certainly the criticism from such figures as Seldon indicates a perception that Thatcher and Major did not go far enough. Devigne (1994) has argued that despite his lower public profile, Oakeshott ultimately had more influence than Hayek, and this might actually have been because he was less radical and more gradualist. Conservatives consider themselves to be pragmatic. One of the themes we pointed to in chapter one, but which is not particularly present in libertarian thought, is a gradualist or managerial approach to politics, so that change is gradual and only occurs when it preserves rather than threatens those institutions that essential freedoms depend upon. Perhaps we should suggest that this essential conservative trait won out over more libertarian impulses.

We can therefore reconcile aspects of the libertarian view—the critique of the state, support for private property and the role of markets—with the conservative disposition. These concepts, particularly the role of markets, were given a higher profile under the Conservatives as a result of the influence of the libertarian thinkers we have considered. But still the basis for this reconciliation was the third element of the conservative disposition, the belief in the necessity of gradual or incremental change. The pragmatic element in conservatism allowed it to adapt and to adopt certain libertarian ideas, particularly those which melded well with the conservative ideas of scepticism towards the state and the support for private property. Therefore might we not suggest that the most important element in conservatism is this pragmatism, which is such that it can reinvent itself to suit the changing needs of the country? This is perhaps not a particularly original position to take, with several commentators arguing that this is the very essence of the Conservative party (see

Ramsden, 1998 for an example).[2] However, there is a more subtle point I wish to raise with a view to the discussion in subsequent chapters when we turn to consider the post 1997 position: does not this pragmatism point to the very strength of the conservative (as opposed to Conservative) disposition? Might we suggest that the conservative disposition is capable of using different ideologies, whether it is libertarianism or social democracy, and absorb elements of them into the conservative world view? If this is the case, it has serious implications for any ideology that tries to tangle with it, and this might pertain regardless of electoral success.

---

[2] Interestingly, Ramsden argues that the Conservative party lost this sense of pragmatism during the Thatcher governments and this accounts for its catastrophic electoral position. Unless and until this is reversed we can hardly gainsay this argument.

Chapter Three

Ideology or Pragmatism?

Who Needs Ideology?

This discussion about conservatism and libertarianism is all very well, but just how much of what politicians do is actually in any way ideological? Are politicians really driven by big ideas, or do they not merely react to circumstances, to what Harold Macmillan famously referred to as 'events'? So when we consider what actually happens in the day-to-day activity of politics, should we be concentrating on ideas or events?

It is interesting that several recent histories of the Conservative party which include the Thatcher and Major periods, for example those of Clark (1999) and Ramsden (1998), tend to concentrate on events and personalities rather than ideas and philosophy. Indeed, as we have seen, Ramsden argues that it is precisely when the party becomes ideologically driven that it falls into difficulties. An exception to this is the analysis of Green (2002) who explicitly looks at the role that ideology played in the Conservative party. Yet it is rather enlightening that Green still chooses to deal with these ideologies by attaching them to particular individuals — Balfour, Thatcher — and particular events such as tariff reform and the Suez crisis.

Ramsden may well have a point when he suggests that the Conservative party's electoral problems derive from the fact that it was 'infected' with a virulent libertarian virus. According to this view, the Conservative party will only recover when it flushes this virus out of its system and returns to the pragmatism that has characterised its history. In short, the Conservative party should concentrate on governing and leave ideas for the opposition to squabble over: one can even take Mill's jibe that they are 'the stupid party' as long as they are actually getting on and running the country.

But, as we saw in the last chapter, there was no shortage of libertarian critics complaining that the Thatcher and Major governments did not go far enough in privatising the public sector and reducing the size of the state. So for some the problem was not enough ideology, that the zeal and vigour of Thatcherism was compromised by the patrician sense of compromise that had held the Tories back in the post war period under Eden, Macmillan and Heath. If only, it is argued, Thatcher had been more radical, or that she had not been toppled in 1990 and replaced by her 'weak' successor. The problem for 'friendly' critics such as Seldon (2005) was that events got in the way and sullied the principles. The problem therefore was a lack of purity[1].

In some ways this is the nub of the issue: do we want purity in politics; do we want ideas to rule over the vicissitudes of everyday politics; or would we prefer a more pragmatic and measured approach to politics? Indeed what would it mean to attempt to implement a purely principled plan regardless of events? As an example, what would it have meant to have allowed Nozick to create his libertarian utopia that we discussed in the previous chapter? How possible would it be to have a plan involving the dismantling of the welfare state, and most government agencies at the local and national level, and just leaving the courts, the police and private charities? This may be desired by libertarians, but it is hard to imagine a set of circumstances where it might be enacted. It would effectively mean that we would have to dismantle the current state and start again. Perhaps the only example of this is, of course, Cambodia under Pol Pot, and this is hardly an advert for successful political transformation[2]. The problem with massive political change, as the history of communism tells us, is that it is not merely disruptive, but often sinks into evil. As an aside, the problem for a libertarian such as Nozick, with his insistence on rights, and side constraints on others to protect these rights, is just how one can implement a libertarian society without violating

---

[1] New Labour found itself facing the same criticism after 1997 when it retained the Conservatives' spending plans and did not increase spending or renationalise the public utilities. But in this case it was only doing what it had said it would do. The problem was wishful thinking on the part of Labour supporters in the media and party members who actually thought that the election of New Labour had anything to do with socialism.

[2] Of course, it is not my intention to suggest any similarity whatsoever between Pol Pot and Nozick's ideas—they could not be further apart. Indeed after writing *Anarchy, State and Utopia* Nozick did nothing actively to promote his ideas or the libertarian cause more generally. In fact he wrote virtually nothing else on political philosophy.

these rights. As Nozick himself has stated, we cannot call on the greater good as justification for imposing libertarianism on people[3].

Perhaps the only way to achieve perfectionism in politics is to restrict ourselves to writing about it. As soon as we start to implement anything then we are forced to compromise. And, as the example of Nozick shows, it is often our very principles — in this case, of non-coercion — that will force us to do so. Academics, quite properly, tend to take ideas seriously and adhere to them, trying to make them as pure and consistent as possible. Philosophers like Nozick will spend years honing their theories and arguments before publishing them, with a view to making them as polished as they can be. As a result philosophers hope that they will have some influence, but perhaps secretly hope that their ideas will be adopted wholesale; that their reasoning and authority will sway politicians into transforming society exactly as it says in the book. But then they wake up and see how politicians actually operate. Politicians need to get elected and accordingly have to respond to opinions other than their own. Therefore, at best, they tend to use ideas, perhaps having only half understood them[4], but only as disposable tools. An idea might be a way of opening up a new agenda, of creating difference from one's opponents or from what went before. So in recent years we have seen New Labour and the Third Way being used to replace Old Labour and 'second way' socialism. As we shall see in chapter six, there is plenty of debate on the meaningfulness or otherwise of the Third Way. But what is interesting is that since 2001 the term 'Third Way' is now only used by academics who are looking backwards. The politicians, however, have quickly moved on to new ground — all the time claiming consistency and foresight, of course — and have found new toys to play with such as 'respect' or 'modern'.

This is not necessarily a bad thing, and we need to ask why we should expect purity in politics. Why are ideas more important than events so that we should ignore the latter and carry on regardless? In political and social theory we can recount what amounts to a definitive position, be it Marxist, libertarian or conservative. Yet we know that 'really existing socialism' contradicted much of what socialism, in theory, was meant to achieve. Of course, in this case the reality was much worse than the theory, and this may lead the theorist to

[3] I discussed the problem of implementing libertarian ideas in some depth in *Housing, Individuals and the State* (King, 1998).
[4] Nozick in his *Socratic Puzzles* (1997) recalled how Republican politicians cooled to his ideas somewhat when they learned that he felt they should apply equally to sexual behaviour and immigration as to the economy.

disown reality, but why should we assume that it is the theory that we take as the arbiter and not events?

Indeed it is precisely this distinction between theory and practice that distinguishes conservatism from other ideologies. What conservatism seems good at is precisely the ability to compromise, to moderate theory to the prevailing current of events. To reiterate on our discussion in chapter one, and as conservative writers such as Oakeshott (1962) and Scruton (2001) have suggested, the principal aim of conservatism is to govern: for a conservative there is 'no purpose beyond that of government' (Scruton, 2001, p. 14). This does not mean that a particular conservative government will have no aims, merely that those ends will be more determined by circumstance than by theory. And if those circumstances appear to dictate a healthy dose of free market economics, as was the prescription for Britain and America in the 1970s and 1980s, then it does not mean this is inconsistent with a conservative approach to government.

Back to Pragmatism

The key to understanding the ideological disposition of conservatism is that it is pragmatic and amenable to compromise. Indeed compromise is of the very essence of conservative governance: one needs to respond to circumstances to guide both polity and community through unpredictable and uncharted seas, where preformed plans and maps may be of no real use. This does not mean that conservatives are rudderless, rather that they are prepared to change direction if and when some big and dangerous-looking object looms in their path: for a conservative the route is always less important than the journey.

I want to draw to a conclusion on the nature of conservatism and move towards the discussion of housing policy, by offering three related principles for Conservative policy making that are consistent with this pragmatic approach. The first principle is that politics is about the practical, and so we therefore have to start from where we are now and not from where we would like to be. Theorists have the luxury of assuming away current institutions, practices and expectations, but only the most driven and ruthless politician would seek to ignore them. It is counter to the nature of conservatism to attempt to tear up the present for some future hypothetical gain. As Scruton (2001) stated, this effectively results in a government being at war with its people, where it uses them as fodder for some utopia that may never be founded.

A Conservative Consensus? 69

In a modern democracy government has to deal with bureaucracies, institutions, traditions and interests, and this presents a huge amount of inertia resisting change and reform. This is not merely because bureaucrats are against change, but also because they have services to provide whilst reform takes place. Any changes have to be incremental and be implemented within a complex set of relationships where the priorities of key players may be elsewhere: head teachers may be more interested in teaching and learning than budgets and human resources. Governing, therefore, contains an inevitable amount of expedience and compromise. We can assume that all politicians know this, but only conservatism makes it into a virtue.

A second principle is what might be called the *Salisbury position* after the Conservative Prime Minister at the end of the nineteenth and start of the twentieth centuries. Salisbury was considered, and perhaps liked to think of himself, to be the most reactionary of prime ministers (Roberts, 1999). However, his position was rather more nuanced than that. The Salisbury position can be characterised as the belief that if reform is inevitable, then it is best carried out by conservatives who understand and respect the key institutions of the state rather than being conducted by zealots or radicals who want to destroy those institutions and replace them with something untried and untested. So Salisbury may have had little enthusiasm for electoral reform in the 1880s, but saw that the only means of 'staving off the mob' was to ensure that the conservatives introduced a 'sensible' set of reforms (Roberts, 1999). The result, of course, of Salisbury's opening up of suffrage was the electoral dominance of the Conservative party ever since. In some ways this is a position taken from Burke and his idea of conservatism being about evolution to preserve those institutions that protect the liberties of individuals.

The third principle, which follows naturally from the second, is the need that conservatives have to defend basic interests, such as property and personal freedom. As Burke (1999) stated, we need to reform institutions to preserve them and to ensure that they fulfil their purpose of protecting our interests. As circumstances change, so must our institutions. But what does not alter is our respect for these basic interests and the need we have to preserve them.

When we take these three together we realise that change will be needed, but when it does need to be undertaken it will be difficult and unpredictable, because of the inertia that exists within bureaucracies and institutions. As a result of this, change should be considered, gradual and piecemeal with the emphasis on protecting what is valuable rather than change for its own sake. Whenever we hear a desire to transform or, more likely, modernise, we need to ask 'what for?' and question the credentials of those who propose the changes.

So might we not conclude our discussion of the ideas behind Conservatism by suggesting that what lies behind the conservative disposition, and what holds it together is this pragmatic sense that we need to manage things as they are and only to change when it is for the best? Conservatism may adapt and adopt different elements as the Conservative party did in the 1980s, but this sense of pragmatism will always hold it in check. What defines conservatism therefore is gradualism, and a sense that there are many different interests that need to be maintained and protected in a plural society that has developed unique institutions and interests. What matters then is that government does things in the accepted manner, and this is precisely what Thatcher, for all her radical rhetoric and controversy, actually did. She almost always stayed within the bounds of both the possible and achievable. Indeed those attempts to be really radical failed badly, the prime example being the flat-rate community charge introduced in 1988 to fund local authority activity. Here Mrs Thatcher badly miscalculated and introduced a policy generally seen as unfair and unworkable, and her successor was forced to withdraw it in a hurry. Where she succeeded though was through incremental changes and making full use of opportunities, such as trade union reform and privatisation. We should remember that privatisation was not a priority in the first term despite it being so central to the second and third terms. But even here privatisation was done piecemeal, one industry at a time, leaving the difficult industries until last. In a similar vein, trade union reform was incremental rather than being carried out in one big reform.

I would suggest that one radical change did succeed in the Thatcher period. But it did so only because it could be fitted so closely into the conservative disposition and thus did not appear to be so radical at all. This policy change was the decision to sell off council houses at a discount and thus fundamentally alter the tenure balance in the country, as well as opening up the opportunities of property ownership to many working people. The Right to Buy policy was certainly radical, and was indeed controversial, yet it is also the most successful and transforming of housing policies. Yet it fitted so comfortably within conservatism simply because it came out of one of the key themes of the conservative disposition. It was, therefore, radicalism designed to achieve a key conservative aim, thus preserving a key interest in furthering personal freedom and autonomy.

We have now fully considered the conservative disposition, and shown how it was able to absorb elements of libertarianism. What we now need to do is to consider how this disposition manifested itself in housing policy. The Right to Buy is perhaps the most prominent area of policy, but it is by no means the only issue we need to consider. The next chapter outlines just what these issues and policies were. It is a consideration of actual policies that will allow us to determine whether there is a consensus formed around the conservative disposition. And so, finally, we move on to housing.

Chapter Four
Conservative Housing Policy

From Ideas to Policies

It is not entirely cynical or lazy to suggest that conservatism is what the Conservative party does. No other mainstream political organisation claims the conservative mantle in the UK, and all of its opponents are keen to make the association. At one level then, the distinction between conservatism and the Conservatives is somewhat redundant. Most politicians are interested in ideas, but they are more interested in power and in doing things. The things that they choose to do might be motivated by ideology, but conservatives also recognise that politics is about achieving the possible, and thus they have to moderate their ideological proclivities according to the political currents of the day. So ideology does not operate outside of political processes. This means that we cannot extricate ideas from action. Politicians want their party to win as that may mean that they are able to implement their ideological programme. But it is also about power in itself, about being able to do things at all. This tribal quality to politics becomes more of an issue with the Conservatives because, as we have sought to demonstrate, conservatism is a disposition or an attitude rather than a fully-fledged theoretical position: conservatism is about governing as such rather than governing to achieve some particular end.

But this has not prevented several commentators from criticising Conservative governments, for not being properly conservative. As we have seen, Giddens (1994), in describing his notion of philosophical conservatism, argues that the Thatcherites were the radical reformers, and trade unions were the reactionaries defending their treasured institutions and practices. According to Giddens, post-Thatcherite politics is not simply about the left as reformers and modernisers whilst the right tries to oppose them. In the 1920s

Chesterton neatly divided the world into Conservatives and Progressives. He stated that 'The business of Progressives is to go on making mistakes. The business of the Conservatives is to prevent the mistakes from being corrected' (*Illustrated London News*, 19 April, 1924). However, we might now argue that the reverse is the case, with the erstwhile progressives desperately trying to hold on to their gains — trade union rights, public industries and so on — and the Conservatives making the changes (and perhaps mistakes). The Conservatives indeed had a definite programme which they sought to impose on the country.

The lament from the left might be, therefore, that if only Thatcher had been more of a traditional conservative and not tried to do so much. But, in their turn, the Thatcherites were critical of the Heath government in 1970–74 for its apparent statism and preparedness to prop up the public sector at the taxpayers' expense (Green, 1987). The Thatcherites therefore saw themselves as returning the party to its true course by rejecting the post-war consensus around an active state, which they argued had led to the long-term decline of Britain economically and socially.

A further criticism has come from traditionalist conservatives such as Scruton (2001), who see no necessary connection between conservatism and capitalism. The criticism here is that Thatcherism was more liberal than conservative in its orientation, paying more attention to thinkers such as Hayek rather than Oakeshott. In justifying this argument, these traditionalists point to the emphasis put on individual freedom and choice, the favouring of markets and the criticism of the role of the state. These values, critics such as Scruton (2001) would suggest, are not conservative ones but those of classical liberalism. This is an issue that we have dealt with in the previous chapters. However, the point here is to emphasise that what constitutes conservatism is contested, and we can make a case for seeing particular Conservative government policies, be they those of Heath or Thatcher, as 'non-conservative'.

This, I would suggest, is neither particularly surprising, nor does it present us with too much of a problem. Conservatism, as we have seen, respects pluralism and we would therefore expect a range of views within conservatism, as well as a toleration of differing views from outside. Moreover, conservatism as a practice is circumstantial, responding to events and problems as they present themselves. We should not therefore expect it to be a homogeneous monolith with clearly prescribed aims, nor should we be surprised that the empha-

A Conservative Consensus?

sis that conservatives place on ideas and practices also changes according to circumstance. This is only a problem if one believes in the purity of ideas over action, which is a view that has made little progress inside most conservative movements.

What I wish to do in this chapter is to consider key Conservative housing policies and to relate them to the preceding discussion on the nature of conservatism. My aim is to develop the three themes identified in chapter one—first, pragmatism, or what I choose to refer to in this context as the pragmatic management of change; second, the critique of the state; and, third, the desire to extend private property ownership—by looking at the influence of these themes on policy. My aim is to show that key housing policies, particularly over the last thirty years have mirrored these key themes. My aim is not to present a complete history of Conservative housing policy, but rather to highlight what I consider to be the most significant issues.

Of course, this is only possible with a considerable degree of hindsight as well as selectivity. I am aware of the possible objection that I have selected on those policies which concur with my identified themes. However, as I shall show in chapter five on policies in the early twenty-first century, the themes of property ownership, pragmatic control and the encouragement of personal subsidies remain at the centre of current debates. So I would suggest that the policies I have discussed in this chapter are truly significant both historically and in terms of their present resonance, and that these policies can be clearly connected to the key elements of the conservative disposition. The policies that I have discussed represent the enduring elements within Conservative housing policy.

I have not restricted my discussion exclusively to the 1979–97 period, although this does take up a considerable part of the discussion. My purpose in the broader discussion is partly to show the consistency and continuity in Conservative thought and how this is manifested in policy making. But I also want to show how arbitrary it would be to place cut-off points—1979, 1997—on discussions of policy making, where new policies build on old ones within an ongoing process of service delivery. Elections and changes of government are important, and they can be used to delineate epochs and be seen as watersheds and so on. But any UK government remains Her Majesty's, and only has different persons running the same departments, with the same civil servants and providing the same services. A housing policy initiated by legislation in 1980 or 1988 remains in force regardless of a change of government. So all that changed after 2nd May 1997 was the furniture in 10 Downing Street.

As we would suspect from the direction of the discussions in chapters one to three, the one theme that emerges as dominant is that of pragmatism. Whilst the Conservatives, particularly post-1979, have shown particular ideological concerns, manifested most strongly in their dislike for local government and support for owner occupation, they have seldom allowed this ideology to turn into dogmatism[1]. What we shall see is that pragmatism will nearly always re-emerge to moderate ideology when it is felt to be threatening the main aim of conservative government, that of governing itself. This pragmatism takes the form of managerialism and an apparent self-interestedness, whereby the role of government, and by that I mean government at the centre, is placed above other interests in the state. I therefore wish to consider this theme of pragmatic managerialism first, to show how far it is ingrained in the practice of Conservative (and conservative) government.

Pragmatism with a Purpose

The welfare state has always been safe in the hands of the Conservatives as, quite simply, they have managed it for thirty-five years of the last half of the twentieth century. Moreover, in two prolonged spells of government — 1951–64 and 1979–97 — they had the apparent opportunity to transform the public sector. They did this with public industries such as the main utilities, transport, coal and steel. However, they did not transform the provision of health and education, which stayed largely as it had since 1945. As we saw in chapter two, classical liberal 'friendly' critics such as Seldon (2005) see this as a considerable blemish on the Thatcher record.

But what about housing? Might we not argue that the shift towards mass owner occupation, the cuts in social housing and the growth of housing associations (a sizeable proportion of this through stock transfers) that took place after 1979 suggest that housing was treated differently from education and health? Might we not say that, in housing at least, the Conservatives actually did transform welfare?

But we can also point to apparently contrary trends running concurrently to this support for owner occupation and demunicipalisation, such as decentralised housing management and the

---

[1] A major exception to this, of course, is over Europe.

development of equal opportunity strategies. It would be hard to argue that the culture of housing was 'conservatised'. Indeed most of the changes enacted by the Conservatives had to be pushed through in the face of opposition from social landlords and the housing profession.

We can explain this, partly at least, by the fact that there is a gap between policy making and implementation. Central government might make policy and develop strategies, but the actual specifics of providing services, particularly in housing, are a local issue. These services have their own culture and are susceptible to their own cultural changes, which might be influenced by central government but are not entirely conditioned by it. Furthermore, this culture might, indeed is likely to be, inimical to conservatism: state employees are more likely to support state intervention and provision than a party that is inherently sceptical of it. Hence we can see trends in the delivery of housing services that appear to run counter to the aims of the centre. This culture does not alter because of the result of a general election and is only influenced incrementally by policy change. This means that we should not expect all aspects of policy in a particular area to be in line with the agenda of the ruling party.

What makes this more of an issue is the fundamental point that we keep returning to, that governments cannot stop the provision of services in order to change them. Local authorities and housing associations have to continue building, maintaining and managing housing even while government seeks to reform them. This means that change is incremental and subject to a considerable constraint. The need to maintain services means that central government has to operate within the existing culture that imbues a particular service, even if it finds it uncongenial. It also offers the prospect that immersing oneself in this culture can lead to one being converted or 'going native' instead of actually doing any converting oneself.

These two factors would in any case lead towards a pragmatic approach to government. One has to use structures and organisations that are already in place and one can only reform or transform them whilst they are being used to maintain services. There would then be a natural presumption towards pragmatism, and this can be seen by the fact that Labour governments have faced the same constraints as Conservative ones.

However, as we have suggested, one of the key elements of the conservative disposition is a belief in government for its own sake, as a necessary activity, rather than one having any specific purpose. As we saw in our discussion of Oakeshott (1962), there is no necessary purpose to governing, but it can and should be seen as a sufficient occupation in itself. This quite naturally leads one to accept the institutions that one inherits and seek to manage them effectively and efficiently. According to this doctrine, one should only seek change if it is the only necessary means to preserve those institutions that one holds dear.

This element of the conservative disposition has a lot of explanatory power, in that it helps us with an apparent anomaly in post-war British politics. The problem is this: Labour in power created most of the welfare state, initiating comprehensive education, the National Health Service and mass council house building. Yet it was only in power for fifteen years of the last half of the twentieth century. For the rest of this period the Conservatives have been in government. We might therefore expect that these state institutions would have been dismantled and returned to the private sector. But this has clearly not been the case. Of course, many socialists would argue that the welfare state has not developed as it ought to have, and is now a residualised and attenuated version of the immediate post-war dream (Malpass, 2005). Yet this still does not account for why Conservative governments, which held power for thirteen years in the 1950s and 1960s and for eighteen years between 1979 and 1997, maintained the welfare state largely intact. Indeed one can go so far as to suggest that whilst Labour created the welfare state, the Conservatives have actually managed it.

The explanation for this, ignoring arguments about how the welfare state would have developed if Labour had both created and managed it, lies in the nature of conservatism, and more particularly, the pragmatism that lies at its heart. The Conservative party was initially hostile to state welfare, and doubtless if Churchill had won the 1945 election the structure of welfare in Britain would have looked very different (Ramsden, 1998). However, having lost that election the Conservative party sought to reassess its policies and attitudes to state welfare. In other words, just as occurred after the catastrophic electoral defeat in 1906, the Conservatives reinvented themselves as a party capable of managing the British state as it had become, and as the British people apparently wanted it. Change may not have been welcome at the time, but the Conservative party has always been good (at least it was until 1997) at recognising that the clock could not be turned back and that a new reality had therefore to be faced. Accordingly, if new institutions such as the National

Health Service and council housing gain general acceptance and are seen to work, the Conservative party seeks to accommodate them.

One way of viewing so-called 'traditional' conservatism is to see it as supporting things as they are now. Chesterton certainly intended to mock when he saw the role of Conservatives as preventing mistakes from being remedied, but there is some truth in the statement. What makes things acceptable, or at least bearable, is that they exist and must therefore have come about for some reason. As we have seen, this has led libertarians such as Hayek (1960) to criticise conservatism for its apparent incoherence—future change bad, past change (now) good—but it does have the advantage of creating stability and questioning why we want things to change. Conservatives are acutely aware that change is accompanied by costs, and that these are unpredictable and one never knows where, and on whom, they will fall. Conservatives will therefore always have an inbuilt bias towards the actually existing rather than the hypothetical (Quinton, 1993).

This pragmatic managerialism we have identified can be seen in regard to two particular housing policies: one that apparently ran counter to property interests, but was allowed to persist—rent controls—and one example of where the Conservatives were able to control and use a practice devised initially to subvert their policies—stock transfer. The first of these policies persisted through much of the twentieth century and had a considerable effect on the viability of private renting, leading to the question of why it was allowed to remain; the other policy is still current and serves to show that the conservative trait for continuity and pragmatism is not merely restricted to one party (a point that will become particularly pertinent as our argument develops).

Rent controls, where a ceiling is imposed on rents which landlords are forbidden to exceed, were first introduced as an emergency measure by the war-time Asquith government in 1915. However, they were not abolished after the war, largely as a result of a continued shortage of housing and inflationary pressures (Malpass and Murie, 1999). Indeed attempts to curtail them in the 1930s by the Conservative administrations under Baldwin and Chamberlain foundered again because of war. A more concerted attempt at abolition was attempted in 1957 by the Macmillan government. However, this policy was reversed and rent controls re-established when Labour returned to office in 1964. Rent controls were abolished in 1989, seemingly permanently in that there is now a consensus amongst the main parties. This, however, did not prevent the Major government from reintroducing non-statutory administrative restrictions on rent levels through the Housing Benefit and subsidy systems (King, 2001).

It has been Conservative governments then that have sought to abolish rent controls. However, it is also important to remember that rent controls existed for much of the twentieth century, which was dominated electorally by the Conservatives. The attempts to abolish these controls were at best spasmodic and could certainly not be said to be a priority for the Conservatives. Moreover, we can suggest that statutory controls were quickly replaced by administrative ones which had much the same effect (King, 2001), but have allowed both Conservative and New Labour governments to maintain an apparently principled opposition to statutory controls.

We need therefore to understand why the Conservatives were prepared to tolerate rent controls for much of their periods in office. Doing so will allow us to understand why they were able to successfully abolish them in 1989, but not before. The first point to make is that the main arguments against rent control were largely liberal or free market ones, rather than being necessarily conservative. As we have seen, conservatives show a great respect for private property, but they do not necessarily connect this with free markets (Scruton, 2001). Accordingly, the key arguments for the opponents of rent control, such as the creation of market distortions, the one-sided nature of their effects (whereby landlords are effectively subsiding tenants at the government's behest) and the disincentive effects of limiting income, were articulated more by classical liberals than conservatives (Albon and Stafford, 1987). Conservatives, it could be argued, had higher priorities than the bottom end of the housing market. Indeed, if one reads histories of the Conservative party such as Clark (1999) and Ramsden (1998), there is remarkably little discussion about housing, with the possible exception of the mid 1950s and, of course, the Thatcher period. Where there is discussion it tends to be limited to owner occupation.

Until the post-war electoral defeat there was still a hangover of the old patrician Tory view that politics should be distinguished between the 'high' issues of foreign policy and defence, and 'low' issues of administration. The belief remained, derived from high Tories such as Salisbury, that there were certain issues that politicians should not delve into and which were best left to local politics (Roberts, 1999). The consequence of this was that the Liberals and, more particularly, Labour were given a clear run on issues such as housing. Housing issues only came to be seen as important within the Conservative party in the 1950s when Macmillan, as housing minister and later prime minister, sought to compete with the Labour party in terms of the number of council houses built (if not, as Malpass and Murie [1999] point out, in terms of quality of dwellings built and rents charged). Housing became important as part of the post-war reinvention of the Conservative party undertaken in reaction to the 1945 election defeat.

The main reason for the maintenance of rent controls, I would suggest, was that there was no real alternative but to maintain them. Conservative politicians realised that of themselves rent controls would not deal with shortages in supply, and might even encourage landlords to withdraw from the sector, as was indeed the case when controls were removed in 1957. The housing minister who saw through the 1957 changes, Enoch Powell, also argued for market rents in the council sector as a necessary change in order to allow the abolition of rent controls in the private sector to have any effect (Shepherd, 1996). However, he was overruled on this and thus the measure failed, partly because there was now a sufficient quantity of good quality council housing available at subsidised rents. Powell, regardless of his reprehensible views on race, was an economic liberal and in some ways the precursor of the free market stream that ran through Thatcherism. He was, however, as Shepherd (1996) points out, very much a lone voice in the Conservative party of the 1950s.

The reason that rent controls could eventually be abolished in 1989 might be traced to a change in political outlook, so that Powell's view was now dominant. Indeed there was an element of truth in this, in that it was felt that higher rents would act as an incentive for private landlords (DOE, 1987). However, I would argue that the main reasons that rent controls could be abolished were rather more pragmatic. Firstly, by 1989 the private rented sector had been reduced to less than 10 per cent of the housing stock. It was no longer electorally significant, paling against the dominance of owner occupation. But secondly, unlike the situation in 1957, there was now a comprehensive system of housing allowances in the form of the Housing Benefit system, that acted a safety net for tenants facing higher rents. The majority of tenants did not suffer as a result of ending rent controls because their rent was paid by government subsidy. This meant that abolishing rent controls was largely risk free in a political sense, if no longer cost-free[2] (King 2001).

We should therefore see the abolition of rent controls as an example of where it was possible to make a *safe* ideological decision. The existence of the Housing Benefit system cushioned the impact on tenants and landlords alike. It allowed the Thatcher government to argue that it was creating a free market, but without the element of risk that one associates with markets. Private landlords did not need to compete against each other, as they could ensure a ready income through accepting Housing Benefit claimants. Likewise, tenants were largely insulated from the effects of higher rents. The Conservatives, as it were, hedged their bets by achieving an apparent freeing up of the market, without the risk of too adverse an impact on any of the players. Of course, the cost of this pragmatism was on their own budget with a tripling of Housing Benefit costs between 1989 and 1996. But they dealt with this by the entirely pragmatic manoeuvre of piecemeal changes to the Housing Benefit system and subsidy regulations to limit rent increases (King, 2001). In any case, private renting, for all the resonance it had for economic liberals, did not matter in political or electoral terms. Elections were not won and lost due to private renting. A greater priority, and one with equally strong resonances to conservative thinking, as we shall see below, was owner occupation.

However, there is a further example of Conservative pragmatism that I wish to consider. This is the manner in which the Conservatives' attitude to stock transfer developed in the 1990s. This is important in that it shows how they were able to mould a practice, intended initially to allow local authorities more freedom from capital restrictions, into a key part of their housing policy. It is also significant in that this policy has been extended by the Labour government into one of their major devices for securing additional spending on housing (DETR/DSS, 2000).

In the early 1990s several local authorities began to explore the possibility of transferring their housing stock to a newly created housing association. This would allow them to avoid the capital finance restriction imposed by the *Local Government and Housing Act 1989*, which forced authorities to use capital receipts to clear debt or to invest them rather than permitting them to use the funds to build or maintain dwellings. Stock transfer would allow these newly cre-

---

[2] It was precisely this increase in costs to government that led to the imposition of administrative rent controls in 1996.

ated housing associations to build new housing and upgrade their existing stock. So this practice of large-scale voluntary transfer (LSVT) can be seen therefore as an attempt to circumvent government control, even if it was at the expense of losing local democratic control over the properties.

However, the policy did not entirely run against government thinking of the period. The *Housing Act 1988* had introduced Tenants' Choice as a means of transferring council housing into the private sector, as well as Housing Action Trusts as a vehicle for private sector investment in poor quality social housing. These policies largely failed, in that they did not win the confidence of tenants (see the discussion on Tenants' Choice below). But still the aim of the government was to transfer council housing into the private or housing association sectors and away from local authority control. It is therefore possible to see the government taking the view that, if its own initiatives were failing, it would instead take advantage of voluntary actions to further its broader aims. Accordingly, in 1993 it took control of LSVT to ensure that this met with the government's aims. An annual quota was established, along with a procedure for approving the transfer and overseeing the process. In addition, a 20 per cent Treasury levy was charged on the receipts from the transfer. This was justified because of the impact of extra available capital receipts for local authorities to use, and because of the knock-on effects on the Housing Benefit budget of tenants moving from rent rebates to rent allowances (King, 2001).

What this quota and levy shows is that the Conservative government was prepared to moderate stock transfer to ensure that this did not jeopardise its other plans. It did not want to see a rapid increase in local authority spending and so imposed a quota on the number of transfers permitted in any one year. It also did not wish to see the Housing Benefit budget increasing as a result of stock transfer. Housing associations were fully reimbursed for the cost of Housing Benefit, whilst local authorities were not. Hence the levy helped to offset the increased costs of Housing Benefit caused by stock transfer. What this shows is that ideology was not allowed to run ahead of the practicalities of government. The Conservatives were quite prepared to use stock transfer as an alternative vehicle in place of the measures they had failed to make work. But they would not do so regardless of the consequences. Their priority was to control stock transfer and to ensure that it worked for them and in their interests.

The policy of stock transfer became the centrepiece of policy in 1996 with local authorities being obliged to consider the option of stock transfer in their Housing Investment Plans (King, 2001). Whilst the Conservatives lost office before this practice took effect, the Labour government has taken it on and indeed extended it. Stock transfer since 2000 has become the main vehicle for new investment into housing, with an annual target of 200,000 dwellings to be transferred (DETR/DSS, 2000). The effect of stock transfer has been considerable. Between 1988 and 2003 970,000 local authority dwellings had been transferred, with over 400,000 of these having been transferred since 2000 (Pawson, 2004). The significant point here is that the change of government has seen no fundamental shift in attitude towards stock transfer. As we shall see in chapter five, the same reasons for the appeal of stock transfer to the Conservatives — of bringing in private sector finance and thus ensuring improvement without imposing great additional costs on the Treasury — have now seen it become the key element of Labour housing policy. The Blair government is seeking to improve the quality of the housing stock without massive increases in public expenditure — despite significant increases since 1997, government expenditure on housing is now back merely to the levels it was in the early 1990s (Wilcox, 2004) — and sees stock transfer as the most effective means for achieving this. Thus, despite its criticism of past Conservative policies, the Blair government is extending them, and this is because it has largely the same aims in mind.

So pragmatism is not unique to the Conservative party and its housing policies. Inasmuch as the Conservatives adapted to the changing circumstances of the post-war period, so New Labour has had to recognise that there is a new consensus that has developed around the support for owner occupation, a limited state, and private sector solutions to social problems. This, as we shall see, is the key to understanding current housing policy discourse.

The Proper Role of Government

This new consensus can be characterised as centring on the belief that the state's resources cannot be called upon to solve all social problems. Indeed the view holds that, in some cases, the state might actually create the problem. This can be seen as a theme developing from the libertarian element within Thatcherism (Green, 1987). Yet as we saw in chapter one, it has a long history in conservative thinking. In particular, there is the view developed by Oakeshott (1962) of the unpredictability of government planning, of the impossibility of rationality in politics. In a similar manner to Austrian school thinkers such as Hayek (1978, 1988) and Mises (1981), Oakeshott believed this to be an epistemological failing: it is just not possible for a centralised planning structure to gain the requisite knowledge to plan effectively. Conservatives have therefore always seen too much government as a problem, and scepticism towards government has been a theme that runs through nearly all conservative thought. Even more traditional thinkers such as Scruton seek to limit the role of government and cavil at attempts to control many traditional activities.

Yet their view can still be distinguished from that of classical liberals such as Hayek and Mises. They do not believe that there should be no role for government, or indeed that the role of government should be limited. What is meant by this is that where it is proper for government to act, it should be able to act without restriction. Oakeshott, as we have seen, was scathing of the effects of vested interests, such as trade unions and the professions, which he thought were trespassing on the relationship between the state and its citizens (Devigne, 1994). According to this view, there should be nothing to clutter up this relationship which would prevent the proper actions of the state on behalf of society and its members. This implies a strong central government, which is precisely what the Thatcher governments sought to achieve, whatever their rhetoric on free markets might have stated (Gamble, 1988). Indeed, as Gamble suggests, it was only through a strong centre, able to clear away all obstructions, that the Conservatives thought that individuals could exercise their economic freedom. What is at issue here, therefore, is just what is the proper role for government. This is the second key theme that we can see in conservative thinking, and we need to demonstrate how it has been manifested in housing policy.

As I mentioned above, it was only in the 1950s that the Conservatives showed any concerted interest in housing as a policy issue. In the 1930s they had reformed building society finance with a view to encouraging owner occupation (Boddy, 1992) and had made some attempts to reduce rent controls. Yet it was only in the 1950s that the Conservatives came to terms with housing as an important social problem, albeit of a different nature from health and education (see below). The more libertarian supporters of the Thatcher governments have tried to characterise Conservative governments in the 1950s and 1970s, particularly under Macmillan and Heath, as in some way soft and reneging on the Conservative legacy (Boyson, 1978). They saw themselves as returning the Conservative party to the 'true faith' and away from a consensus based on social democratic institutions. In some way, it was argued, the party had become sullied by compromising with state intervention. This is now a rather arcane argument, politics having moved on from the heady days of the Thatcherite ascendancy. However, whilst there may be some merit in the criticisms of the Heath government in particular, the Thatcher period cannot justifiably be called one of government retrenchment. What occurred rather was a period of very active and radical government — government with a purpose which was thus, as it were, very un-Oakeshottian — seeking to free individuals from the dead hand of the state. The Thatcherites did not wish government to stop doing things as such, only those things they did not approve of. And, perversely, the vehicle that would achieve this shift in focus was central government itself.

The main way in which this shift has been manifested in housing policy is through the restriction in the role of local authorities and the move towards personal housing subsidies. This change shows both the attempt to change the role of government, and the increasing centralisation of control in the hands of the centre. Despite the Thatcherite critique of the Heath government between 1970–74, the first concerted move in this direction began in 1972 with a major attempt to reform the funding of local authority housing. The *Housing Finance Act 1972* made three important changes, all of which have had lasting effects. First, it ended the discretion local authorities had traditionally enjoyed over rent setting by extending the 'fair rent' system already in operation in the private sector. The aim of this policy was to increase rents considerably, thereby allowing subsidy to be reduced. Whilst this particular measure was abolished in 1975, it saw the first attempt to focus housing finance away from government subsidies and towards rents, thus limiting government's subsidy liability.

The second change was the replacement of all existing government subsidy liability with a new deficit subsidy which was calculated annually on the basis of a local authority's income and expenditure. The previous subsidy system, which had remained largely intact since 1923, paid a fixed amount per dwelling for a fixed period of years. The aim of this was to assist councils in paying off their borrowing incurred in building new housing. The effect of the 1972 act was that government was no longer committed to particular levels of subsidies into the future; moreover, it now had leverage over rents in that it could make certain assumptions on rent levels when setting the annual subsidy. Government now had a mechanism by which to control activity, in that a reduction in the level of subsidy would necessitate an increase in rents.

The third change was no less important, seeing the introduction of a mandatory rent rebate scheme for council tenants and tenants in non-furnished private rented accommodation. The significance of this change was that ability to pay was no longer a bar on access to council housing. All households could now afford council housing. Over time this change, coupled with the Right to Buy, has done more than any other to alter the nature of council housing. Rent rebates have allowed the very poorest to gain access to council housing, but the Right to Buy has denuded the tenure of the best quality and most popular housing and the most affluent tenants.

The importance of the 1972 Act then was, firstly, that it gave government a mechanism by which to control activity, but secondly, it saw the start of the move away from object subsidies to subject subsidies. Since 1972 this policy has continued. Further restrictions on local authorities were imposed in the *Housing Act 1980* and the *Local Government and Housing Act 1989*, both of which led to increases in rents through a reduction in subsidies paid to local authorities (Malpass, 1990; King, 2001).

The effect of these pieces of legislation was to alter the balance of government support. In 1976 over two-thirds of subsidy was paid out in the form of bricks and mortar or *object* subsidies. These were aimed at allowing local authorities and housing associations to provide new additional housing at subsidised rents. It was felt that the best way to deal with a housing shortage was to offer financial incentives to encourage social landlords to build dwellings. The main effect of these subsidies therefore was to increase the *supply* of housing. The remaining third of housing expenditure was paid out in the form of tax relief to owner occupiers and rent rebates. These are referred to as *subject* or *personal* subsidies. The aim of these subsidies is to make housing more affordable by increasing household income. They therefore have the effect of increasing the *demand* for housing.

However, this balance between object and subject subsidies has now been almost totally reversed, with over 67 per cent[3] of subsidies now in the form of subject subsidies (Wilcox, 2004). Throughout the 1980s and into the early 1990s mortgage interest tax relief (MITR) to owner occupiers had increased dramatically from £2.2 billion in 1980/1 to a peak of £7.7 billion in 1990/1 (Wilcox, 2004). Since then MITR has declined and was completely phased out in April 2000. But since the late 1980s Housing Benefit has increased and more than replaced the cost of MITR to the Treasury. In 1988/9 the total cost of Housing Benefit was just over £4 billion, but by 2003/4 the figure had climbed to £12.6 billion. (Wilcox, 2004). At the same time gross revenue and capital subsidies to local authorities and housing associations had fallen, with Wilcox (2004) estimating a real-term decline in direct expenditure on social housing between 1980/81 and 2001/02 of 67 per cent.

This may mean that in real terms government spending on housing has altered little, but the change in the effect of this expenditure has been considerable. Subsidy now encourages demand, and is predicated on the basis that there is no great shortfall in housing supply. As we shall see in chapter five, the Blair government in its *Sustainable Communities Plan* (ODPM, 2003) appears to be beckoning a 'step change' in demand-side housing expenditure. However, the increases in planned government expenditure are relatively small if one looks over the long term, with much of the promised investment to be provided by private finance.

This shift in policy over the last decade can be seen as a shift away from municipalisation and towards individualised provision. Instead of the state providing housing according to its priorities, individuals are to be assisted in their own decision making. Instead of subsidies to social landlords, the majority of funding is now in the form of support to individual households. The aim is that individuals should now be able to choose where they live, free from the dictates of the state.

But, of course, the system does not operate in this manner. The majority of Housing Benefit recipients are social housing tenants, living in dwellings that have been built with state subsidy. Indeed

---

[3] The increase in housing expenditure under new Labour has reversed this trend somewhat, with the percentage of spending on subject subsidies in 2001 being at 71%. However, assuming government sticks to its announced expenditure plans there will be little further shift. In any case what has had more influence has been the relative stability of Housing Benefit expenditure since 1996.

taking a sufficient number of Housing Benefit recipients guarantees social landlords their income and allows them to meet their business objectives (King, 2001). In addition, the Housing Benefit system, because it is means tested, and therefore alters with income, actually creates the sort of dependency it is meant to end (King, 2001). This is because benefit is withdrawn as income rises, thus reducing the incentive to take up low-paid employment.

The problem here is that governments, both Conservative and Labour, have not been prepared to loosen their control over housing subsidies. It has been more important to maintain spending at manageable levels than to allow the subsidy system to properly free up household choices. Thus when gross Housing Benefit expenditure increased dramatically in the first half of the 1990s, the Major government introduced a range of measures to restrict this increase. This ranged from the limiting of subsidy to local authorities to the restriction of entitlements of young single people (King, 2001). The Conservative government was therefore not prepared to allow a market in rented housing to develop freely. This would have necessitated either an open-ended Housing Benefit commitment from government or a fundamental reform of the system, both of which it refused to do (King, 2001).

This raises the other side of these reforms, namely, the accretion of power at the centre. As a result of the various housing acts discussed above and further measures introduced since 1997[4], central government now has virtual control of the income and expenditure of social landlords. It can dictate what is spent on maintenance and improvements, as well as setting rent levels. But this was justified by the Conservatives in the 1980s and 1990s on the grounds that local authorities were not acting responsibly and were jeopardising national targets (Jenkins, 1995). However, despite the noises made by Labour in opposition, it has continued with this policy of centralisation and extended it considerably. Jenkins (1995) sees the policies pursued by the Conservatives as a contradiction. They were trying to enhance individual freedom by increasing the centre's control over resources. He complained that the policies of Thatcher and Major would merely provide an incoming Labour government with a ready-made structure for state planning. Indeed, we can suggest

---

[4] As we shall discuss more fully in chapter five, the Decent Homes Standard, which dictates levels of expenditure, and rent restructuring, which sets target rents to be achieved for all social housing units, are the main post-1997 policies.

that this has happened, although the Blair government has still found the need to extend it further.

However, returning to the conservative disposition, we might question whether there was really any contradiction here. The question, I would suggest, turns on whether one sees the Conservative governments between 1979 and 1997 as being libertarian, and therefore placing free markets and individual freedom at the forefront of their policy making, or as being more true to their conservative roots. My view is that the desire to maintain control actually shows an Oakeshottian view of government. Conservative policies on housing do demonstrate a concern for individual freedom, but within a framework of a strong enabling state. These policies seek to rid the state–citizen relationship of those encumbrances which the Conservatives would consider detracted from the legitimacy of the state as an enabler on behalf of its citizens. Hence, intermediate institutions such as local authorities have found their roles circumscribed, whilst the expectations placed on individuals have increased.

So, as with the discussion on rent control and stock transfer above, the Conservatives were not prepared to develop the policy towards personal subsidies to its ultimate. The overriding instinct for conservatives is towards pragmatism, to ensure the survival of government itself. Accordingly, policies are attenuated to ensure that problems do not get out of control, even if this means a degree of apparent inconsistency with the government's avowed aims. Government for a conservative is an end in itself and policy is always to be subservient to that. That is Oakeshott's particular insight, and what the Conservatives under John Major appeared to forget, as they seemed all too intent on believing their own rhetoric and acting upon it.

Property

The main ideological statement by the Conservatives on housing was the White Paper, *Housing: The Government's Proposals*, published in 1987 (DOE, 1987). In this paper they juxtapose the apparent inefficiencies of the social sector, with its unresponsive bureaucracy and lack of choice, with owner occupation. So, unlike the housing association sector, which they claimed enjoyed over-generous state subsidies which could no longer be justified, government supports to owner occupation should be maintained. According to the white paper this was because:

> Home ownership gives people independence; it gives them a sense of greater personal responsibility: and it helps to spread the Nation's wealth more widely. These are important factors in the creation of a more stable and prosperous society, and they justify the favourable tax treatment accorded to borrowing for house purchase by owner occupiers. (DOE, 1987, p. 2)

It was therefore justified for government to support owner occupation, even though one of the avowed aims was to inculcate greater personal responsibility and independence. Thus one can concur with Forrest and Murie (1988) when they suggested that 'The owner occupied sector has become a state sponsored, subsidised sector rather than a deregulated private sector' (p. 234). This policy of state support was maintained in opposition to the more market-oriented strand within the post-1979 Conservative government which argued that tax relief distorted the market, creating unnecessary lurches in demand.

But it is noticeable that the white paper does not rely on liberal arguments to justify advocating government support for owner occupation. Whilst it does mention independence, it also refers to the spreading of wealth and the creation of stability. As we saw in the discussion on property in chapter one, it is precisely the linkage between property and social stability that makes ownership so congenial to conservatives. And, as we saw with Scruton's discussion of property, it is seen as incumbent on conservatives not to ensure that property can be hoarded by the few, but that its benefits be distributed as widely as possible across a society (Scruton, 2001).

It is, of course, true that the level of state sponsoring of owner occupation has declined with restrictions placed on the Right to Buy and the abolition of tax relief on mortgage interest. Yet this has not seen the end of state support for owner occupation (it still enjoys exemptions from capital gains tax, as well as the general zero rating of VAT on housing which benefits all tenures). What I would suggest rather is that this change of tack in the early and mid 1990s was another example of the pragmatism we have already discussed as a key theme in Conservative housing policy.

But it is also the case that the Conservatives offered support to owner occupation prior to 1979. This has led some academics to suggest that there was no real transformation in policy in 1979 (Forrest and Murie, 1988). Their argument is that owner occupation had been an important element of policy for many years prior to 1979 and that housing, unlike education and health care, had never been decommodified: the market still played the majority role in housing in contrast to health. The implication of this argument is that housing *could* have been decommodified if there had been the political will to do so. However, it is my contention that the issue was not one of political will. It was not just the case that politicians did not get around to it, nor was it even a matter of the expense of nationalising the private rented stock. The issue was rather that it was never a practicable consideration to do this, and this was precisely because of the particular role played by property. Indeed the gradual understanding of this role, no doubt hastened by increased affluence particularly amongst working class households, has led to the further commodification of housing in policies such as the Right to Buy. I would even go so far as to suggest that it was the recognition of this desire for ownership that formed the particular genius of the modern brand of Conservatism developed by Thatcher and her colleagues (King, 1996, 2004). The Conservatives in the 1970s recognised the resonance that property had to aspiring working class households, and tapped into this. Therefore, whilst previous governments had supported owner occupation, it did not have the centrality within policy making that it achieved after 1979.

In discussing the importance of owner occupation to the Conservatives — and to show the linkage with the conservative understanding of the importance of property — I wish to contrast two Conservative policies pursued since 1980 — the Right to Buy introduced in 1981 and Tenants' Choice introduced in 1989 — and show why one succeeded and the other failed. Both these policies were intended to achieve the privatisation of housing and diminish the stock of local authority dwellings, and to give the residents more control.

The Right to Buy had been one of the key elements of the Conservative's election manifesto in 1979. It allowed council and non-charitable housing association tenants to purchase their dwelling at a discount. The initial policy insisted on a 3 year qualification period (later reduced to 2 years) with a maximum discount of fifty per cent (later increased to sixty per cent for flats)[5]. The effects of this policy have been considerable and well documented (Forrest and Murie, 1988; Malpass and Murie, 1999), with over 1.5 million tenants exercising their right to purchase. But the policy did not merely reduce the number of properties; it also reduced the aggregate quality of the sector, with a disproportionate number of family houses being sold, leaving unpopular flats on less desirable estates. In addition, the

---

[5] Both discounts and qualifying periods have been restricted since 1997.

1980s saw an increase in homelessness that can be partly attributed to the shortfall in properties suitable for families (Pleace *et al*, 1997).

Tenants' Choice was intended to be the next 'big idea' from the Conservative government after the Right to Buy. By 1987 the majority of tenants seeking to exercise their Right to Buy had done so, and consequently the Thatcher government looked to further measures to reform social housing. The aim of Tenants' Choice was to allow council tenants, acting as a group, to force a ballot to determine a change of landlord for their estate. The new landlord could be an existing housing association or a new body formed for the purpose. Somewhat controversially, tenants choosing not to vote in a ballot would be assumed to be in favour of the transfer (King, 1996). There was a belief within government that council tenants would leap at this opportunity to change landlord. However, only one group of tenants succeeded in changing landlords and this was in the Conservative-controlled London Borough of Westminster, and was in response to a proposal from the borough to sell the estate to the private sector. The only lasting significance of this policy, as Malpass and Murie (1999) indicate, is that it established the notion of tenants' voting for a change of landlord which, as we have seen, became a feature of housing policy through stock transfer.

So one policy succeeded and, despite its knock-on effects, was undoubtedly popular with tenants, whilst the other failed to capture the imagination of tenants. The reason for this, I would suggest, is that there is a fundamental difference between the two policies. The Right to Buy recognised and built on the fundamental relationship between a household and their closely held things — between household and home — whilst Tenants' Choice dealt merely with the relation between landlord and tenant. The Right to Buy, which allows sitting tenants to buy their current dwelling, focuses attention on housing as a private entity, whilst Tenants' Choice, which allowed council tenants as a group to vote for a new landlord from an approved list, retained the perception of housing as primarily public. The Right to Buy alters the relation between an individual household and *their* dwelling by vesting control with the household itself. However, Tenants' Choice, if it had actually been used, would have left the relation between dwelling and household unchanged, merely altering the landlord. The tenants would now merely be beholden to someone else, and the fact that they could have a choice of whom to be beholden to would not materially affect their own level of control. Any power the tenants had would be lost as soon as they had voted, but this is precisely when the landlord's power over them would begin.

The distinction here, therefore, is that one policy concentrated on the use which the household could make of the dwelling — it became an asset and something they could pass on to their children, use as collateral, sell for a profit, take a pride in owning, etc. — whilst the other was concerned with the ownership of a collection of dwellings. One policy, through allowing households to exercise greater control, succeeded, whilst the other failed to capture the imagination of tenants, largely because it would not change anything beyond whom they paid their rent to. The essence of the Right to Buy as a successful policy, therefore, was the fact that it played on the private relation between a household and the dwelling: it concentrated on the internal relation by which the household could control their environment.

What is germane here is the increased level of control experienced by households exercising the Right to Buy. Their subjective experience of the dwelling has been altered because they are now able to exert a more fundamental influence over their dwelling environment, including even when to change it by moving to a new dwelling. The dwelling has therefore been privatised, in that it is no longer legitimate for the public to have an interest in it: it is now the sole responsibility of the resident household to maintain it, pay for it and to determine its use (King, 2004).

With this sense of control comes responsibility, not only for the thing owned but also for what it encloses. It is in this sense that the policy of the Right to Buy was quintessentially conservative. It acted on the presumption that ownership is the primary social relation that gives meaning to things around us. It brings with it freedom to act, but also the responsibility for the consequences of these actions (Scruton, 2001). In this sense, we should see this as the most conservative of housing policies.

But it was only a part of a policy aimed at extending owner occupation further across the population, with the eventual aim of eighty per cent of households attaining it (DOE, 1995). The Conservatives gave consistent support to owner occupation during their period in office, especially through the use of tax relief, which peaked at £7.7 billion in 1990/91 (King, 2001). Likewise, when the housing market slumped in the early 1990s, the reaction of the Major government was not to promote rented housing as a possible alternative, but to use public funding to shore up the market (King, 1996, 2001). Hence it devised the so called Housing Market Package in 1992/3 to allow housing associations to buy up empty properties with the aim of stabilising the market again. The support for owner occupation was by now so ingrained that any alternative could not be countenanced (King, 1996).

It is by now an idle speculation to try to link the slump in the housing market in the early 1990s with the sustained period of unpopularity of the Conservatives. Clearly there were other issues at work — sleaze, over-familiarity and, most of all, the debacle of the Exchange Rate Mechanism linking sterling to other European currencies — yet we cannot deny the effect that the slump in the housing market had on the public's view of the competence of the Major government.

But this period in the early 1990s is also interesting in that it saw a significant change of tack in policy towards owner occupation. The Right to Buy remained and owner occupation was still seen as the tenure of choice (DOE, 1995), yet increasingly the role that government saw for itself changed, from one of direct intervention to effect change to a more hands-off approach with the aim of ensuring stability in the housing market (King, 2001). We can date this change in direction to 1993 when Kenneth Clarke became Chancellor of the Exchequer. He took the view that the Housing Market Package had been a waste of money which had merely benefited private developers, and not individual households in financial difficulties. Moreover, there was now ample evidence that government policy might actually have the effect of destabilising housing markets. This was partly because of the effects of subsidies, which served to encourage demand and led to periodic shortages in supply.

But the main reason for the change in policy was a broadening understanding of the embedded nature of owner occupation in the wider economy. Government now appeared to grasp that what mattered most was not tax relief, but secure employment prospects, stable interest rates and low inflation. What the housing market needed from government was economic stability so that house prices did not rise too quickly and that mortgage rates were stable and affordable. The most noticeable manifestation of this new policy was the phasing out of MITR which began in 1994 and was completed by the Blair government in 2000. Indeed the most succinct explanation of this new approach, initiated by the Conservatives, can be found in the 2000 green paper, which states:

> The main contribution government can make to sustainable homeownership is a robust economy in all parts of the country and a strong system of consumer protection. As a result of our economic policies, homeowners are benefiting from relatively low mortgage interest rates and rising living standards. ... We are determined to avoid a return to the boom and bust economy of the past, which eroded the security many expected from their homes and created an uncertain climate for one of the most important long-term financial commitments which most people make. (DETR/DSS, 2000, p. 30)

If we accept that this has been the broad thrust of policy towards owner occupation since 1993, we can draw two conclusions. First, despite the ideological predisposition towards property ownership, the conservative disposition of pragmatism and governing for its own sake again comes to the surface. If the political and economic circumstances alter, then the conservative approach is to change with it. This was the case with housing policy in the 1990s. If the Thatcherite policies that had worked in the 1980s no longer seemed to be appropriate, then these should be changed. This did not mean any diminution in the importance placed on owner occupation, rather that it now needed to be supported in a different manner. As a result the sacred cow of Tory housing policy — the belief that tax relief could not be withdrawn — was slowly starved to death, and apparently without anyone really noticing.

What this suggests, as we have seen already, is that ideology is not allowed to override pragmatism; or, put another way, the Conservatives have always provided for a considerable degree of leeway within their principles to allow for changes in circumstance. The policy towards owner occupation is no exception to this. The Conservatives maintain their support for owner occupation — as do all the mainstream political parties — but when they felt that one set of policy instruments were failing, they were prepared to shift to something they thought would be more successful. This, of course, did not prevent them from receiving a heavy defeat at the polls in 1997. But that election did not turn on housing policy, and in any case there was little that the Tories could have done to turn public opinion around. What it did do, however, was to shift fundamentally the debate again and create a new set of parameters within which owner occupation was discussed.

This takes us to second point. The change in position taken by the Conservatives in 1993 has formed the basis for owner occupation policy ever since. As the quote above from the 2000 Green Paper shows, the Blair government has merely continued with this policy of stability. This might be seen as the lack of inspiration of the Blair government, or the low political priority given to housing. These are all charges that one could legitimately level at the Blair government, but the point I wish to make here is somewhat different. What this continuity shows is that there is something in the very nature of property ownership that is now almost universally recognised (amongst politicians if not academics!). This is that property ownership connects to some elemental core in individuals. It resonates with them in some inchoate way, which commentators can no longer wish away simply as the result of politicians bribing tax payers with their own money. Put another way, the institution of property ownership is now so embedded that it cannot be rationally opposed. In this sense it can be said to be part of the conservative disposition, with which, at the meta-level, politics has now properly come to terms. We should therefore not be surprised that both Conservative and Labour parties now appreciate the importance of owning property.

There is a sting in the tail though, and that is that something so important and so popular means it forms a tempting target for politicians. Thus, as we shall explore in chapter five, one of the consequences of a decade of stability coupled with an appreciation of a deeply-held desire for property ownership is that politicians cannot ignore it, but rather seek to capitalise on it. Hence, we are perhaps seeing the re-emergence of a more interventionist attitude towards owner occupation with the Blair government's thinking emerging in its *Homes for All* strategy (ODPM, 2005). But what is fascinating about this strategy, which seeks to extend owner occupation to those who currently cannot gain access to it, is that it appears almost exactly to mirror Scruton's point that the aim for conservatives is to extend property ownership to all to ensure that they all have a stake in the culture of the country.

Conclusions

This chapter has indulged in a rather selective treatment of history, choosing particular policies in order to substantiate a point, or rather several points. My aim has been to show how key conservative ideas have manifested themselves in housing policy. This has indeed been selective and not really much of a historical survey at all. However, in mitigation — and I consider this to be a knock-down argument — we have only to look at what is the focus of current housing policy. If we do this, as we shall do in the next chapter, we see that owner occupation is still central to policy, with government seeking means of sustaining and extending it. We can see that the emphasis is still on private sector solutions to solve housing problems. We see that government is seeking to extend choice in housing instead of leaving it for state institutions to decide, and is aiming to do this partly through the use of Housing Benefit as a demand-side incentive.

But what we also see is a sense of pragmatism, of continuing with those policies that have worked in the past (even as one denigrates their inventors), and the attenuation of apparent principles in order to maintain the greater principle of government being in control. Thus we hear of 'step changes', but without any huge change in resources (ODPM, 2003), and we hear of the extension of choice without any change in structures (DETR/DSS, 2000). Perhaps more fundamentally we see private sector solutions being paraded as enhancing social justice and inclusiveness. What we have then, as we had before 1997, is housing policy being conducted within a conservative framework by politicians who (apparently) understand the virtues of a conservative disposition. This, of course, is a controversial statement and so it is what I shall now try to justify.

Chapter Five

Housing Policy After 1997

New Labour, freshly elected on a bright sunny May morning in 1997 set about fulfilling a key pledge — to spend only what the Major government had decided to spend over the next three years. Despite the sense of a new beginning, of freshness and the opening up of possibilities, the new government, under its young and energetic leader, consciously and deliberately followed the plans of its predecessors. Just how significant should we see this? Were those who witnessed the first morning of Blair's premiership deluding themselves — or being deluded — when they thought that some great change had occurred with the first Labour election victory in twenty three years?

But then, the New Labour government — and it definitely wanted to be known as 'new' — was merely doing what it had promised. When it insisted on the prefix 'new' this was not to differentiate itself from the Thatcher and Major governments, but to distinguish itself from 'old' Labour, from its socialist past and the idea that it would be a government that increased taxes, renationalised the privatised utilities, and invited trade union leaders to tell it how to run the country. The sense of being 'new' was its recognition that the country had changed since the 1970s and that the old nostrums of left/right politics had changed.

But this begs the question of what had changed and who had done it: just what was it that the revamped Labour party was responding to? It is my contention that New Labour's response was not just to the failure of Old Labour — and after four successive election defeats the failure was palpable — but to what had inflicted those defeats. What had led to the creation of New Labour was the success of conservatism in remodelling the political landscape so that to call oneself a socialist in public was electoral suicide.

In this chapter and the one that follows, I wish to look at post-1997 developments. My concern quite obviously is with housing, and so I have chosen to begin with a discussion of housing policies since 1997. My aim, by having this chapter following my discussion of Conservative housing policies, is to demonstrate the continuity, the basis for a consensus. Having done this I shall then consider what this tells us about the Blair government, whether it is a 'third way' between old-fashioned socialism and a supposedly outdated conservatism. What I hope to show is that much of what has happened in housing policy since 1997 is a mere continuation of the Thatcher and Major years. The priorities have not altered, nor have the mechanisms to achieve them. Where there has been a shift it is in emphasis, particularly in the centralisation of resources and political control. However, it is still possible to discern the same themes and imperatives that have driven housing policy since the early 1980s. The question that I shall need to answer is whether this centralisation has had the effect of subverting the conservative disposition we saw embedding housing policy up to 1997.

As in the previous chapter I do not admit to being comprehensive, or to discussing the issues as fully as I might. My aim is to provide the broad brush strokes that allow us to see the outline and some of the patterns within. In this way we can identify the ideological underpinnings without getting bogged down in the minutiae of policy. I am aware that selectivity can lead to the accusation that I am loading the evidence to prove my point. However, the policies I discuss in this chapter are not marginal or insignificant, but are central to the Blair government's thinking on housing. This may indicate that New Labour has been content for its predecessors to do its thinking for it, but nevertheless this is where housing policy is going.

The Key Themes

The years either side of the new millennium have hardly been quiet ones for housing, with a lot of apparently new initiatives being announced and implemented. The basis for this activity was laid out in the *Housing Green Paper* (DETR/DSS, 2000), the *Sustainable Communities Plan* (ODPM, 2003) and the five-year strategy, *Homes for All* (ODPM, 2005). Whilst these changes involve an increase in expenditure on social housing, there is also a heightened emphasis on choice. The specific mechanisms to be introduced involve an enhanced use of stock transfer to lever in private finance, the regulation of rent levels, the reform of housing allowances and an increase in support for owner occupation. These measures involve an apparent increase in commercial disciplines to enhance efficiency, but also a greater level of central regulation, so that all social housing has to meet a common standard of amenity by 2010, and submit to a national rent-setting formula that effectively determines the income of social landlords. One result of this standardisation through centralisation is that social housing has effectively been turned from a local to a national service, with central government assuming the role of planning for its use, financing and improvement.

There is much that is familiar here from the discussion of Conservative housing policy in the last chapter. What we need to do immediately therefore is to separate out the level of activity from what is new and distinct. Whilst there is much happening, I want to suggest that not much of this is based on original thinking, but is rather a continuation or an extension of Conservative policy, as is seen by the use of stock transfer, the emphasis on commercial disciplines and the use of choice-based mechanisms.

It is my contention that New Labour housing policies can be characterised by three themes. First, as I have already mentioned, they have centralised the governance of social housing to the extent that it is now perceived as a national asset, with an emphasis placed on the element of national resources used to fund them rather than local resources and purposes. Second, they have expanded social housing provision, but at only limited additional cost to the Exchequer. As we can see in table 1, planned expenditure as a result of the *Sustainable Communities Plan* does not significantly increase from the levels of the 1990s.

What this shows is that the government can only claim a 'step change' in housing expenditure by comparing planned expenditure with the actual expenditure in its first term. Wilcox (2004) shows that if we convert these figures to real terms (at 2001/02 prices) the resources for the Sustainable Communities Plan only return expenditure to the level of the first three years of the 1990s. Indeed Wilcox shows that if housing expenditure in 2000/01 were to match 1990/91 levels it would need to be at £6.7 billion and to match spending in 1980/81 it would need to be at £14 billion. In fact spending in 2000/02 showed a fall of sixty seven per cent compared with 1980/81. Therefore it appears that the government needs to take many steps even to match the 'bad old days' of the Thatcher governments.

Table 1: Total Housing Expenditure, 1990–2006[1]

Year	£ billion
1990/91	4.9
1991/92	5.8
1992/93	6.3
1993/94	5.3
1994/95	5.3
1995/96	5.0
1996/97	4.6
1997/98	3.7
1998/99	3.7
1999/00	2.9
2000/01	3.1
2001/02	4.6
2002/03*	5.4
2003/04*	6.5
2004/05*	7.5
2005/06*	7.7

* Sustainable Communities Plan

What New Labour has done is to use public funds to draw in private finance. In particular, private sector borrowing has been used to fund the expansion in housing association development, as well as the improvement in the quality of social housing through the use of stock transfer, arms length management organisations (ALMOs) and the private finance initiative (PFI). The important point here is that government is able to claim the benefits of increased expenditure—or as it erroneously terms it, 'investment'—without incurring the extra expense itself. This is, of course, a situation that also pertains to its capital programmes in health, education and transport. What is important here is that this practice of using private finance to fund public sector projects is an extension of the sceptical approach to state involvement we have picked out consistently in conservative thought and action. What may be different here is that New Labour is not merely using this as a mechanism for improving effi-

---

[1] Sources: ODPM (2003); Wilcox (2004)

ciency, but to achieve extra investment without it impacting directly and immediately on the Treasury.

The third theme, and the one that might be seen at first glance to be original to New Labour, is the development of policies to deal with differential demand between regions and tenures, and hence growth areas, market renewal areas and the use of social housing to expand owner occupation which are part of the *Sustainable Communities Plan* and *Homes for All*. The significance of this policy is that it points to housing and planning policies that are more embedded into the broader economy. As Clapham (2005) has pointed out, housing policy has shifted away from assisting the poorest to managing demand and access consonant with differential labour market pressures in the North and South of the country. Whilst this seems a break with the past, if only with the admission that there is indeed a North/South divide in terms of employment and housing that needs to be dealt with, we might also see it as a case of thinking on social housing catching up with thinking on owner occupation since 1993. As we saw in chapter four, government since the early 1990s has seemed to understand more fully the manner in which housing is embedded in the wider economy, and hence has concentrated on broader economic policies than specific housing based actions. The policies coming out of the *Sustainable Communities Plan* might be seen as an extension of this thinking to include social housing and the planning system.

But, whatever the originality of policies dealing with differential demand, the first two priorities can clearly be seen as extensions of pre-1997 policies. Stock transfer was becoming increasingly significant in the latter years of John Major's government, which also saw the first attempts to use the Private Finance Initiative (PFI) for housing (King, 2001). Therefore, little has altered in the direction of policy since 1997 other than the scale of activity, in terms of direct government spending and the use of stock transfer and the PFI. I would also suggest that there is little evidence to believe that much would have changed if a Conservative government had been elected in 2005. What has changed is not so much the direction of policy, but the speed of change towards centralisation and risk aversion by the Treasury.

With regard to the relative significance of these three themes, I would suggest that the dominant theme is that of centralised control. We have already seen that the idea of a strong central government was one of the central principles of Thatcherite conservative ideology that dominated government in the 1980s (Devigne, 1994). Instead of seeing institutions such as local authorities as playing a positive role in the development of policy, the Conservative governments saw them as one of the causes of Britain's post war economic and political decline. The Conservatives believed that Britain was becoming ungovernable because of the diverse demands being placed upon the state by groups such as the trade unions, and institutions. There was perceived to be a breakdown in central authority. Thus a key role for government was to reassert the authority of the state in the face of these competing demands. We can see the effect of this in the public and social policies of the Thatcher governments, which circumscribed the power of the trade unions in the nationalised industries and public sector; these policies also tried to deal with the professions such as teaching, and constrained the spending and activities of local authorities which could be seen as an alternative source of power.

What is particularly interesting here is that, whilst New Labour's rhetoric may be rather different from that of the Conservatives, it has not sought to alter the relationship by returning powers to the local level. It has found the centralisation of the 1980s and early 1990s rather congenial to its style of government. Indeed whilst the Conservatives oversaw a considerable increase in power for the Treasury, it has reached something of a peak under Gordon Brown's chancellorship, with much of social policy appearing to derive from the Treasury rather than the specific departments of state. Housing policies since the late 1980s, when the government insisted that capital receipts be used to pay off debts and introduced private finance for housing association development (King, 2001), have been determined for the convenience of the Treasury, with strict controls on public spending and limiting of liabilities through risk transfer to the private sector. The effect of this has been to keep significant amounts of borrowing for social housing 'off balance sheet', but without losing control of the assets. This has been achieved by an increase in regulation with bodies such as the Housing Corporation having a more interventionist approach to housing association governance, despite disbursing fewer funds to a smaller number of associations. The result is a series of hugely complex and bureaucratic mechanisms: so, for example, choice-based lettings have to be imposed and rent targets established rather than rents being determined by demand, and landlords being allowed to respond by demolishing unpopular housing and replacing it with better housing in areas of high demand.

So even though the last decade has seen an increasing use of private finance, this has not been a period of liberalisation. Indeed it is not too far-fetched to argue that local housing providers are now almost completely controlled by the centre. This is achieved through a series of policy mechanisms that now largely control the income and expenditure of social landlords, and which determine where new developments will be built and by whom. Now this trend over the last decade was not something invented by New Labour, but, as Jenkins (1995) predicted, it is something that those believing in active government would love to get their hands on.

The important point for the argument in this book is whether this greater emphasis on centralisation subverts the conservative disposition: does centralisation become so dominant that the pragmatic managerialism that it sprang from is destroyed? In addition, does this also damage the other two themes of scepticism towards government and support for the individual, and encouragement of property ownership? I shall answer this question in the next chapter, but first I need to garner the evidence that will allow me to reach a conclusion.

A Plan of Their Own?

Governments, of course, only do things for a reason. Accordingly, it is certainly possible to see current policies as being linked by some common purpose. The government suggests that this purpose is to improve the quality of social housing and to allow for greater choice and opportunity in the sector. As a means of achieving this they are attempting to create rent convergence between all social landlords; introduce choice into the lettings process; ensure that local authorities plan for the long term and make effective use of their assets; improve quality by imposing a common standard of amenity; and reform Housing Benefit. But there is also a different purpose, which is to ensure that government maintains control over social housing and can thereby achieve its objectives without any adverse effects on the public purse, and I believe that we should see these policies in this context.

Of course, it is rather easy to see patterns and suggest that they are all part of some grand plan. However, in this case, the government is quite explicit that these policies are linked, and indeed many of them have developed out of the 2000 Housing Green Paper (DETR/DSS,

2000). This does not mean that the policies will succeed in their intentions, but I feel that we should take the government's intentions at face value, and so I intend to look at these policies and how they link together.

Rent Restructuring

This is a national rent setting policy that largely determines the income of social landlords. It should be seen, amongst other things, as a form of administrative rent control, in that it sets target rents that social landlords have to achieve by 2012. Indeed rent restructuring is rather more prescriptive than the statutory controls that were abolished in 1989.

Rent restructuring can be seen as an attempt to restrict rent increases. However, it also aims to achieve some comparability across all social landlords in a locality. The government argues that 'choice in social housing is distorted when rents differ for no good reason' (DETR/DSS, 2000, p. 5). One of the aims of the policy, therefore, is to 'reduce unjustifiable differences between the rents set by local authorities and by registered social landlords' (DETR/DSS, 2000, p. 93), presumably so that applicants can make informed decisions. Housing association rents in 2000 were on average 20 per cent higher than those of local authorities and the government felt that there should be some convergence. Moreover, they felt that rents should be set in both sectors according to the same principles, using a formula combining property values and local earnings. The idea therefore is that similar properties in a locality will have similar rents, rather than differing according to the type of landlords. The advantage for the applicant, it is argued, is that once social housing rents are comparable within a district it will then be possible to make comparisons between local social landlords in terms of quality and management, rather than between costs which have arisen as a result of different subsidy systems and rent setting policies.

In some ways we can see rent restructuring as the logical extension of the administrative rent controls the Conservatives introduced in 1996. By effectively setting a target rent for each and every dwelling owned by social landlords rent restructuring can exercise control over income, as well as creating more predictability over Housing Benefit expenditure. Rents can be effectively controlled and this can be achieved on a permanent basis, and according to a standardised process that is administratively straightforward for government (but not for social landlords who are forced to administer the process at their own expense).

But there is a problem with the policy. Information on quality and management is precisely what applicants will lack, unless they have already experienced several local social landlords in the past. Thus the mechanisms determining choice are likely to be reputation and marketing, rather than any accurate assessment of the particular service being offered. What has been expressly removed here is what could act as the main signal to quality, namely price. Rent restructuring makes price competition impossible through the bureaucratic imposition of target rents based on common national criteria. Therefore the customer has no ability to make any trade-off between price and quality[2], but must effectively take both these as given. As a result the criteria used to choose between landlords are likely to be arbitrary and based on stigma and local reputations. This, of course, assumes that local demand conditions allow for any realistic choices in the first place. As we shall see, the choice agenda depends on the availability of options on the supply side, so that an applicant could trade off one offer of accommodation against another. One would have to be particularly ignorant of current supply conditions in many parts of the country to believe that this is actually the case.

So it is very debatable whether rent restructuring will enhance choice in any effective manner. One can argue that the reason why it will not work is precisely because it is such a centralised system which offers little or no flexibility at the local level. But this may be precisely what was intended, because what rent restructuring does is to give government considerable control over the incomes of social landlords. Indeed, the use of target rents with a cut-off date to achieve convergence means that social landlords now have a particularly clear notion of their income until 2012. This is one side of what can be seen as a pincer effect whereby social landlords are forced down particular routes by the mechanisms the government uses to control them.

Decent Homes Standard

The other side of the pincer, which affects the expenditure side, is the Decent Homes Standard. Like rent restructuring, this is a policy that affects the behaviour of social landlords in the long term by setting

---

[2] Interestingly, the Blair government is using precisely this trade-off in its Housing Benefit reforms by the use of 'shopping incentives' which provide an incentive to shop around for cheaper rents.

their priorities towards stock improvement above all other areas of activity. In effect, the prescriptions laid down by the Decent Homes Standard inform social landlords of their obligations in terms of dwelling standards and quantify the cost of improvements needed to attain this standard. To meet the Decent Homes Standard each dwelling must, first, meet the current statutory minimum standard for housing; second, be in a reasonable state of repair; third, have reasonably modern facilities and services; and, fourth, provide a reasonable degree of thermal comfort. In many ways this is the key component in the government's strategy for social housing in that achieving the Standard by 2010 drives the decision making of social landlords. The starting point of the policy is for landlords to inspect and value their stock (something which local authorities had already undertaken as part of resource accounting: see below). As a result landlords are now able to apply a benchmark to their stock, in terms of current valuation and survey data, and to relate this to the government's expectations of what standards ought to be. They are therefore able to cost the necessary remedial action needed to meet the standard.

The Decent Homes Standard, taken together with rent restructuring, means that the government now exercises considerable control over the activities of social landlords and is able to determine both income and expenditure. But there is a further policy, specific to local authorities, which exerts yet more pressure.

Resource Accounting and Business Planning

This policy actually predates the two already discussed, having been proposed in 1998 and introduced in 2001. Resource accounting can be seen as attempting several things. First, it recognises officially what had long since been the reality, that the role of local authorities had now changed to that of managers and maintainers rather than developers. Resource accounting recognised this by shifting the emphasis away from historic debt incurred in asset formation (the cost of house building) to a form of accounting that records the current value of their assets. This means that each authority has to be aware of the condition of the stock and the amount of money needed to improve it. Resource accounting can be seen as an attempt to 'measure on a consistent basis the resources used over the lifetime of houses, rather than simply the cash spent on them each year' (Malpass and Aughton, 1999, p. 34).

The government intends that resource accounting will make local authorities more businesslike in their operation and encourage them to manage their assets more effectively. Accordingly, they are now expected to submit annual business plans for their housing revenue account[3]. These plans will indicate how the authority intends to use and enhance its assets over a period of up to thirty years. Indeed the political aim of business planning is to ensure that local authorities are clear about the nature and scale of the problems facing them and what options are available to them. It forces local authorities to concentrate on long-term planning and the need to maintain and improve their own stock.

It is this need for long-term planning that is the really significant part of this housing revenue framework, and this becomes clear when we link it to the previous two policies. The limitations of rent restructuring mean that local authorities know what income they have at their disposal until 2012. The Decent Homes Standard informs them of what they must do to improve their assets by 2010. There is therefore no opportunity for ignorance on the part of landlords about the scale of the problems facing them. For many local authorities this means a deficit between their projected income and their necessary expenditure. They are therefore forced to consider means of addressing this shortfall, and for this the government has given them the three options already referred to of stock transfer, establishing an arms-length management organisation (ALMO), or the private finance initiative (PFI). All of these measures involve the use of private finance.

Private Finance

Housing policy since the late 1980s has undoubtedly depended on private finance in order to meet successive governments' aims. As we saw in chapter four, this was begun under the Conservatives in 1989 who altered housing association funding to predetermined grant rates to be topped up with private borrowing. At the same time, many local authorities began to transfer their entire stock to newly formed housing associations as a means of circumventing government restrictions on the use of their capital receipts. This too used private finance to purchase the dwellings and to improve them. Between 1988 and 2003 there was an injection of £26 billion of private finance into social housing, compared with government expendi-

[3] This is the account that deals with all income and expenditure on the authority's own housing stock.

ture on housing associations in this period of £24 billion (Wilcox, 2004). Private finance has therefore allowed for a doubling of housing association activity over and above what it would have been if it had relied solely on government subsidies. So, the first reason for this policy is that it has allowed for an expansion of activity without huge costs to the Treasury. Private borrowing by housing associations does not count as public borrowing, and thus does not add to the public debt. We can, therefore, see why the transfer of council housing to housing associations has such an appeal.

But, as we have seen, the use of private finance was also intended to alter the incentives operating within public sector organisations. Borrowing from commercial lenders would ensure greater value for money and efficiency in social housing. Social landlords would have to be more cost-conscious and businesslike in their approach. They would be encouraged to plan more for the long term because they were now committed to long-term debt financing. The language of the Conservatives has been moderated somewhat by New Labour — it is now more likely to talk of 'social entrepreneurialism'[4] — but the essential elements of policy have remained and even been developed. What has altered since 2000 is the scale of the use of private finance and the emphasis placed on stock transfer as a key vehicle to meet government policy objectives. While the Conservatives operated a quota limiting stock transfer to 25,000 properties per annum for much of the 1990s, the 2000 Housing Green Paper increased this to a target of 200,000 per year, a target which has largely been maintained (Pawson, 2004).

Stock transfer is clearly the government's preferred option for social housing. The effects of business planning, and the control of income and expenditure, have exerted pressure on local authorities to make fundamental decisions in the knowledge that most will not receive sufficient resources to meet the Decent Homes Standard by 2010. The effect is that much of the cost of stock improvements is therefore funded privately, but without any diminution of government regulation.

However, there are two alternatives to stock transfer open to local authorities. High-performing local authorities — i.e., those meeting most of the government's performance indicators — can seek to establish an ALMO. In this case a separate management company is set up to manage and improve the housing stock. Additional funding is available from government for ALMOs and, subject to an

---

[4] See the discussion on New Labour's language in chapter six.

inspection regime, they may be allowed to borrow at higher levels. As with stock transfer, an ALMO needs to be approved by a tenants' ballot and is subject to a bidding procedure, and needs the sanction of the Secretary of State.

Another alternative to stock transfer, which avoids losing democratic control, is the PFI. The PFI began in the mid 1990s as a means of using private sector finance and expertise in the public sector. It is a means of transferring risk from the Treasury to the private sector by undertaking large capital projects 'off balance sheet'. This means that these capital projects do not appear as public borrowing. A PFI is funded through revenue over a thirty year period, for which government credits are available, instead of the traditional system of capital funding where the full cost would fall completely on the Treasury. So the PFI does not involve up-front borrowing and thus large-scale projects can be funded, with politicians taking the credit, but without any effect on government spending and borrowing. A PFI needs government approval, and this has added to their complexity, with both the Treasury and the private service provider seeking to ensure that they are insulated from risk. As a result a large PFI scheme in Camden was halted by the ODPM in 2005 on the grounds that it carried too much risk and did not represent sufficient value for money. Importantly, therefore, a PFI still needs central government approval before it can go ahead. The PFI is perhaps most applicable when tenants refuse to sanction a transfer, or where the local authority wishes to retain ownership but cannot meet the required performance standards.

The fallout of the use of private finance has been, and will continue to be, significant. But this policy, which predates 1997 of course, is actually based on something of a myth. Successive governments have argued that using private finance has introduced commercial disciplines. Social landlords, it is said, need to operate as businesses rather than as welfare bodies. They have to ensure that they can meet their liabilities and manage their assets. But social landlords are still very far away from being fully risk-bearing businesses. Social landlords still hold a monopoly over local provision, and as associations merge and local authorities transfer their stock, the number of local providers diminishes and the level of local influence they have increases. In addition to this, the level of regulation by government and its agencies such as the Housing Corporation has been extended greatly under the cloak of apparent privatisation. Housing associations are not free to dispose of their assets, increase (or decrease) their rents, or even determine who they house. Most housing associations are still dependent on central government funding, and thus must accept this detailed and prescriptive regulation. Yet instead of being under democratic control, they are accountable only to themselves and the government agencies that fund them.

The net effect of this combination of private finance and centralised control has not led to any liberalisation: there is little or no competition between providers, and little opportunity for innovation and variety without government sanction. Instead of liberalisation, what we have is a situation of greater dependence on government and an emphasis of central control. In addition, what has been consistently eroded is any sense of democratic control of housing assets and any local political accountability. Accountability is upwards, towards regional and national bodies established by government, and no longer to the local community.

The question, however, is how far the liberalisation of social housing was ever intended to go. If the Conservatives had followed the advice of libertarians they would have completely privatised council housing (Seldon, 2005). One could, of course, argue that the Conservatives did actually attempt this in the Right to Buy, the problem being that it depended on the sitting tenants being willing and able to take up the offer. They also brought forward proposals to transfer council stock to the private sector in 1988 with Tenant's Choice, and we have discussed the reasons why this failed so badly in chapter four. What the Conservatives did not do was to encourage competition between social landlords, which might have had the effect of liberalising social housing more effectively by opening up the sector to choice. But this would have taken extra resources, in that competition could only be effective given a sufficient supply of social housing. Instead the Conservatives were more concerned with ensuring that they had control over social landlords, and this has been carried forward by New Labour.

Sustainable Communities Plan

The third key theme is the most current, namely that of dealing with differential demand. As I have already suggested, The *Sustainable Communities Plan* is concerned with developing growth areas of new housing development in the South where the demand for housing and house prices is both high and rising, and the regeneration of abandoned and low-demand housing areas, involving mass demolition, in areas of the North and Midlands. The common theme to these two approaches of growth and renewal is the idea of 'building' communities, be it from scratch or by reinvigorating depressed areas. The result is that the bulk of new housing investment is being targeted at these areas, with the effect that being included in a growth area or a housing market renewal pathfinder has considerable consequences for local housing organisations. Moreover, the shift to large-scale and volume development favours large regional or national housing associations and has led to a rush to join housing consortia or merge to form a larger body capable of competing successfully for volume building.

What ought to be readily apparent is that the *Sustainable Communities Plan* is consistent with the centralisation of policy we have seen as so significant in the post-1997 period. The growth areas and pathfinders are determined by government, which controls the agenda and establishes the rules for development. Hence the significance of the ODPM's insistence that sixty per cent of new development should employ 'innovative' building techniques rather than allowing social landlords to develop in the manner they choose. More than any other, this policy shows that social housing has been 'nationalised', so that government feels that it can determine the allocation of resources and target them as it sees fit.

This has an important consequence in that housing policy has shifted from being uniform and consistent across the country (albeit with some diversity of tenure patterns, rents and access opportunities) to national, in the sense that it is no longer consistent across the country, but directed from the centre to meet particular targets and aims based on national strategies. Social housing policy is no longer about ensuring a consistent coverage of housing, but is instead about chasing notions of 'demand' rather than 'need'. However, this idea of demand is not based on local market signals, but on the assumptions of the planning system and the imposition of central house building targets, derived from what are inevitably out-of-date demographics. The result is the imposition of housing in certain areas regardless of the wishes of the local community, alongside the compulsory purchase and demolition of dwellings in other areas as they are deemed superfluous and which are apparently not compatible with the government's notion of 'community'. As a result, many actually existing communities in the North of England are blighted by the threat of compulsory purchase and demolition leading to a self-justifying atrophy. Indeed the establishment of housing market renewal pathfinders in certain areas such as Hull (John Prescott's constituency) has led to increasing house prices as property speculators buy up derelict properties in the knowledge that they will be compulsorily purchased for considerably more than was paid for them.

The *Sustainable Communities Plan* can therefore be seen as a rather incoherent attempt to impose a model of diversity devised by the centre on localities that have no choice but to accept it. Likewise, social landlords, entirely dependent on government funding and, cowed by regulation, have no alternative but to join in this spurious game of 'building communities'.

This policy is perhaps the most severe example of centralised policy making. It pays little regard to local conditions, yet can have quite fundamental effects on a local area if it is included or excluded in a growth or market renewal area. The *Sustainable Communities Plan* might therefore be seen as the case where centralisation begins to override all other considerations, with the government effectively treating social housing as a national resource to be manipulated and arranged according to a central plan. A policy such as this appears to show a particular confidence in centralised planning entirely at odds with Oakeshott's scepticism of political rationality. As such we might have to doubt whether housing policy retains much of the conservative identity. However, a more recent policy might be said to rebalance things slightly, even if it does not exactly signal a less activist role on the part of government.

Homes for All

This initiative, announced in early 2005, might be seen as the first public recognition by government that social housing has become almost superfluous. This policy involves the introduction of a *First Time Buyer Initiative* which allows 15,000 low-income households and key workers to buy an equity share in their dwelling, many of which will be built on public land; a competition for developers to bid to provide houses at £60,000, again using public land; and an initiative called *Homebuy* for social housing tenants to enable them to buy, at a discount, an equity share in their dwelling of between fifty and one hundred per cent. The Government suggests that this will make owning affordable to around 300,000 tenants.

Of course, the dominance of owner occupation is by no means new, nor is the preparedness of government to use social housing to further owner occupation, as we have seen in our discussion on the Right to Buy. What is different, however, with the *Homes for All* agenda is that the justification was not so much that of independence or even choice, but social justice. The government's argument was that low-income households deserved access to owner occupation as much as the more affluent who already had ready access. Traditionally, of course, social housing was justified on the basis of social justice, and this was the case as recently as the Commission for Social Justice (1995; and see Brown, 1999). However, the view of government is now to divert resources away from social housing and towards owner occupation *in the name of social justice*. Of course, we might see a more cynical motive in this policy, which appears to prioritise households for subsidy based on the electoral significance of the part of the public sector they are employed in.

But, as I suggested in chapter four, we might also see this policy as roughly consistent with the conservative disposition. Scruton (2001), as we saw in chapter one, suggested that property ownership was elemental to social relations and to our understanding of ourselves as social beings. It enclosed the primary social relation of the family, which is a fundamental part of the social order. Accordingly he states:

> Given their belief in the political importance of the family, and their reliance on family loyalties in forming respect towards an established political order, [conservatives] must desire the distribution of property through all classes of society, in accordance with whatever conception of household might be generic to each of them. (Scruton, 2001, p. 95).

It is doubtful that Scruton would describe his as a social justice argument, but we can still see his words here as justifying the *Homes for All* policy of extending owner occupation to all classes. So whilst this policy suggests a more interventionist approach to owner occupation, with all the attendant dangers that may have for the health of housing markets, we can also see this policy as being a particular example of the conservative disposition. It recognises the attraction of owner occupation for the vast majority of households and seeks to ensure that as many of them as possible are able to attain it. In this regard it is a more worked-out version of the Conservative's aspiration, announced in the 1995 Housing White Paper (DOE, 1995), of owner occupation reaching eighty per cent of households.

As I have suggested this might act to balance the apparent rampant centralism of the *Sustainable Communities Plan* and its nationalisation of housing. But when taken together we might need to be a bit more nuanced in our assessment of these two policies. The *Sustain-*

able Communities Plan can be seen as an attempt to plan for growth in certain areas and to facilitate the provision of new owner occupation and social rented dwellings in these areas. However, the chosen mechanisms to achieve these aims differ somewhat according to tenure. On the one hand, funding is being directed towards these growth areas and consequently other areas are being relatively starved of funding. But on the other hand, we see a liberalisation and simplification of the planning regime in these growth areas to assist private developers in building dwellings for sale. So whilst the policy is very much top-down, it does operate differently according to tenure with owner occupation being facilitated whilst social housing provision being directed. Seen in this way, the *Sustainable Communities Plan* fits rather more comfortably with the policy encouraging owner occupation.

Choice

One possible alternative explanation to centralisation as the most significant element in New Labour housing policy is the encouragement of choice. Indeed, this certainly features heavily in their rhetoric and may well be the one concept they would light on as the defining characteristic of their policies. Yet, like the use of private finance and centralisation, the emphasis on choice predates 1997 and has been an important part of housing policy, particularly in terms of the promotion of owner occupation. However, it is my view that choice-based policies, whatever the rhetoric, are subservient to the main focus of centralised control. As an example, the government announced 'targets' for choice-based lettings in April 2002, which required that twenty five per cent of local authorities should have such a system by 2005, and one hundred per cent by 2010 (Brown and King, 2005). This statement was made during the life of the twenty seven pilot schemes established to look at the viability of various schemes, and prior to the large-scale evaluation exercise of these pilots that was not published until 2004 (Marsh *et al*, 2004). This suggests that the policy of choice-based lettings is a 'top-down' initiative that seeks to impose a particular agenda on social landlords, tenants and applicants.

Choice is being promoted by the government, but households and housing providers are only being offered choice on the government's terms. Proposals such as resource accounting and stock transfer might have the proclaimed aim of enhancing local autonomy. But the government is always there to tell housing organisations what they should do with their autonomy. More generally, in the emerging public policy literature on central-local relations in the UK, the phrase 'earned autonomy' is gaining ground (Pratchett, 2002). This emphasises the fact that the current government's priorities are clearly articulated and understood by local authorities and housing associations, and will be driven through by a mixture of 'carrot and stick' incentives and regulations. Autonomy will be earned through meeting performance targets but will still be heavily circumscribed.

But then one can question whether these policies really have anything particularly to do with empowerment and individual decision making (Brown and King, 2005). Instead current choice-based policies seem more aimed at controlling supply side activity, in directing what landlords are doing and the quality and quantity of their provision. As an example, choice-based letting does not alter the demand side, in that choice is still controlled and rationed by the landlord rather than the purported decision-maker (the tenant or applicant). This system does not alter the supply of housing, nor does it change the conditions for accessing housing, in that 'need', as determined by the landlord using government's 'best practice', still forms the main criterion to access the housing register. The aim of this system is to improve the efficiency of social landlords. As the former Minister for Local Government, Nick Raynsford, commented:

> Meaningful choice does require an adequate capacity and the shortage of supply in some services is still sometimes used as an excuse for not permitting users any choice ... However ... the absence of choice may well lead to greater inefficiencies by allowing providers to ignore market signals about what works and what doesn't, so perpetuating outdated and inefficient ways of delivering services. (quoted in Corry, 2004, p. 18)

In some ways this is quite an incredible quote. What Raynsford appears to be saying is that we should not prevent customers from experiencing choice merely because there is nothing for them to choose! But this is because choice-based policies are really being driven by a demand to increase efficiency — as a weapon to 'modernise' public services — rather than empowering individuals.

This misuse of choice can also be seen in the area of Housing Benefit reform. In the name of individual empowerment, the government seeks to reform the Housing Benefit system so that all payments are made to tenants, who therefore become responsible for their rent payments. In addition, instead of tenants receiving their full rent they will get a local housing allowance which will allow them to 'shop around' (DWP, 2002). However, there appears to have been very little thought given as to the effects of changing the manner in which Housing Benefit is paid. In particular, there is no attempt to advise, guide or train tenants with no history of paying their rent. This is a hugely important point in that over seventy per cent of social housing tenants currently have their rent paid direct to the landlord, and many of these will be low-income households who have never paid their rent themselves before. Ensuring that tenants respond properly to these changes will need considerable management, as is shown with a voluntary pilot by London and Quadrant Housing Association, which found that, within 6 months of allowing their tenants to receive payments, arrears had risen by three hundred per cent. This leads to the suggestion that the main impact and effect of the Housing Benefit reforms will be on landlord behaviour, especially in the private rented sector, where landlords can choose to let to groups other than benefit claimants.

Choice is therefore being used merely as another bureaucratic mechanism that controls the activities of social landlords, whilst offering no real prospect of empowering households. One only has to consider how choice sits with other policies to appreciate the real intent. If a private landlord finds one of their properties is unlettable they might decide to lower the rent: in the social sector this is not permitted because of rent restructuring. If a dwelling cannot be let a private landlord might choose to let the property run down, so saving them money: in the social sector the Decent Home Standard applies and the property has to be improved to this standard whether it is in demand or not. In the private sector a landlord can sell the property if he or she chooses and reinvest the proceeds in something else; in the social sector a property can only be sold with the approval of a government agency and any subsidy received may have to be returned. A private landlord can let to whom he or she likes: in the social sector, even with choice-based lettings, a landlord must give priority to groups defined in legislation as homeless or vulnerable. Finally, from the tenants' perspective, in the private sector there is perhaps some prospect of shopping around, but in the social sector under choice-based lettings, the landlord decides if you can bid for a dwelling and decides if you deserve to get it. Choice in the social sector is therefore very much hedged in by other policies aimed at ensuring that landlords do what the centre expects of them.

A Conservative Consensus? 119

The way in which choice does manifest itself in housing under New Labour, just as it did under the Conservatives, is through owner occupation, and what it is important to realise about this is that households exercise their choices *outside* of the influence of government. As the Major government proved in the early 1990s, governments can adversely affect housing markets by their interventions, and as the same government proved, it can help things immensely by leaving housing markets alone (King, 2001). Most households are able to provide for themselves and do, and where they benefit from government it is through the stability that comes from government being cautious and steady on the tiller. There was one phrase that was used on three separate occasions in the 2000 housing green paper and this was, 'Most people are well housed' (DETR/DSS, 2000, pp. 7, 15, 20). This, we should remember, was in a policy document trumpeted as 'the first comprehensive review of housing for 23 years' (DETR/DSS, 2000, p. 5). I think we can legitimately ask what we should make of such a comprehensive review, the first apparently for a generation that concludes that 'most people are well housed'. Ignoring the fact that the Green Paper was a rather timid affair compared to the 1987 White Paper (DOE 1987) that brought in private finance and abolished secure tenancies, and setting aside the fact that the Green Paper did not actually present anything as far-reaching as the Right to Buy that led to the sale of 1.5 million council dwellings, just what does it say about any government that opens its major statement on housing reform by saying that not much is wrong? What I would suggest is that what this statement really amounts to saying is that the majority should get on with providing their own housing because they appear to be doing it rather well.

What New Labour housing policy really amounts to, therefore, is the attempt to control the small and reducing social sector so that it does not become a liability, and if it can be used to support and assist in furthering owner occupation then all to the good. The real focus, however, in terms of active support and encouragement is that very conservative idea – indeed what Honderich (1990) saw as the defining characteristic of conservatism – of promoting owner occupation. In the next chapter I want to consider what this says about New Labour and then make some comments about the nature of the conservative consensus I have identified in housing policy.

Chapter Six

But is it Conservative?

Back to the Conservative Disposition

In the first part of this book I undertook an examination of conservatism and then applied this to housing policy with the aim of demonstrating how the conservative disposition had influenced policy. I then sought to show what elements of Conservative housing policy has been continued and what was changed by the New Labour government after 1997. But what I have not done, as yet, is discuss in any detail just what New Labour is. This is important because British politics does not exactly revolve on housing policies. This area of public policy does not win, or lose, elections, nor is it usually at the forefront of political life. I have considered, implicitly at least, some of the reasons for this in the introduction and at the end of the last chapter, when I discussed the essentially private nature of housing and how it can insulate us from government. Allied to this is the relatively small size of social housing in comparison to owner occupation. But this does present a potential problem, in that if housing is not central to the political process, how can we be sure that what happens in this area of public policy is replicated elsewhere, and particularly in those areas that are more politically and electorally significant? In short, is housing policy typical of New Labour, or is it an aberration?

We have already seen the areas of continuity in housing policy before and after 1997. These can be summarised as a belief in pragmatic managerialism, which has manifested itself since the mid 1990s in particular as a desire to centralise housing policy; scepticism for state provision and the support for individual choice; and, support for owner occupation. Housing policy can therefore be summarised very succinctly in just three words: *centralisation, choice* and *property*.

But as we saw in chapter five, there may be some change in emphasis between the Conservatives and New Labour, with one leaning more on one element than was the case with the other. The element that New Labour has taken up the most, which it has found most useful from the 1979-97 period, was exactly what was predicted by Jenkins (1995), the central control of resources by the Treasury. It has used the levers created by the Conservatives to pressure local government into a particular direction. Despite the rhetoric of 'modernisation' that is never far from the lips of New Labour politicians, it is still not clear what the purpose of this centralisation is. There are certainly the structures in place for centralised socialist planning—the Major government made sure of that—it is just that New Labour does not appear to want to be particularly socialist. When pressed, New Labour politicians and their supporters tend to see their purpose as modernisation, but seem unaware of the ironic nature of this answer, wherein modernisation is seen as justification for modernising.

We saw that thinkers such as Oakeshott (1962) and Scruton (2001) described the conservative disposition towards governing as an end in itself. Just as there is no external purpose to loving someone, to friendship or to fly fishing, so there is no external purpose to governing. Existing and continuing as a community is sufficient unto itself, in that the aim of most people is to live well now and in the immediate future rather than to see their role as providing the means for a future political community to thrive. Might we not see the centralisation of the instruments of government by New Labour in this light? It suggests that it seeks to create a 'modern' Britain, but seems unable to say what this will involve: what constitutional arrangements will be made, for instance, with the House of Lords or the rights of Scottish MPs, and how will public services be reconfigured? The reality, therefore, is that New Labour acts as any other government does: getting through crises and problems, dealing with issues piecemeal, compromising to do at least something rather than nothing, and generally exhibiting extreme caution. In this regard it is rather 'old' in its behaviour, if not in its rhetoric. However, it is not acting as 'old' Labour, but 'old' Tory: what we see exhibited by the Blair government is the form of pragmatism that Conservative governments prided themselves on before the Thatcher period (and, of course, this is exactly the same comment we have made about the Thatcher governments, where actions often did not match the stridency of the rhetoric).

In terms of explaining this situation I would like to suggest three possibilities: the first, and most obvious, is that Blair and New

Labour are indeed conservatives, if not Tories in the tribal sense. They may still feel allegiance to the Labour party, but their core beliefs are actually conservative, and hence we should not be surprised about the level of continuity over the last 20 years. The second possibility is that Thatcherite Conservatism was so successful that no other options are now possible, whether Blair agrees with it or not. After the successes of Thatcher the electorate simply will not accept any alternative other than to go along the same path. The third possibility is that pragmatism dominates now as it did before 1997 and that, despite the tribal nature of politics, there is actually quite a consensus over the direction of the country and how it should be governed. Accordingly, despite the Blair government's rhetoric that seeks to differentiate itself from its predecessor and opponents, it is clear that there is no great need for change, and the disputes between the two main parties are historical rather than substantive. What we might have then is a period that is relatively non-ideological.

Whilst not all these three possibilities can be correct they might not be mutually exclusive. I would suggest that the situation which does pertain is nearer to the third possibility, of a relatively non-ideological pragmatism. Yet, of course, this begs the question of a consensus over what? Hence we might suggest that there is now a period of non-ideological pragmatism because of the success of Thatcherism, which has made the socialist alternative unthinkable. New Labour actually therefore has only limited room to manoeuvre because of the successes of the recent past (the second option) just as the Tories in the 1950s and 1960s were hamstrung by the Atlee reforms of the immediate post war years, which created a high degree of consensus without seemingly affecting the tribal nature of two-party politics. So to succeed as a politician in twenty-first century Britain one needs to be a conservative, at least of the small 'c' variety.

This returns us to the discussion in chapter one on the conservative disposition as an ideology, and what form this might take. It was argued that this disposition might take three forms: we could see the disposition as disinclination to change; as a tribal association such that whatever the Conservative party does is conservative; and, as a condition that permeates a political culture. What I wish to suggest is that we might seem to be able to characterise New Labour by this sense of the conservative disposition as *the cultural condition of politics*. These elements we have noted as being essentially conservative pervade the British political culture, so that any political party must operate within it if it desires any electoral success. A political party, because of its tribal allegiances, and because of the exigencies of events, will tend to emphasise different elements, and as important as any other factor will be the impact of the immediate past. But this happens within a general framework that continues and which therefore allows one political party to take up directly from the other, with practices and policies that are both understandable and readily translatable.

This suggests that conservatism has a high degree of adaptability. The question is, however, just how far can we take this notion of conservative pragmatism? Might there be a danger in seeking to suggest that politics is everywhere and always conservative, merely because of the extent of continuity that exists? First, I would want to suggest that there is much more conservatism about than academic and media commentators will often credit. If we accept the dispositional quality of conservatism I have presented here, this leads us towards the view that it is embedded deeply in most institutions and ideas, just as Giddens (1994) claimed to sense with his discussion of the 'philosophical conservatism' of trade unions, environmentalists and even Soviet communist party leaders. This might not be a fully-fledged ideology, and those who exhibit it might not want to see themselves in the least bit as conservative, yet this sense of an inchoate association with the past and the tried and trusted is exactly what conservative thinkers have tried to pinpoint when they have articulated the special quality of conservatism as an ideology.

Second, we need to recognise that there are different types of conservatism, which have different emphases. We saw this in chapter two when we discussed the influence of libertarianism in the 1980s and 1990s. But being circumstantial, conservatism does take many different forms according to the institutional arrangements of a country be it the Catholic Church as in France and Italy, or the mixture of fundamentalism and individualism that make up conservatism in the USA. However, what underlies them is a common understanding of human nature, and it is this that is pervasive rather than any particular set of institutional arrangements. But third, we need to appreciate that the only thing we are discussing here is the set of institutional arrangements in one country. It is therefore not too unreasonable to see a conservative disposition as being capable of explaining much within that country's political culture.

However, adaptability might work both ways. Inasmuch as conservatism can, as it were, 'infect' other ideologies and parties, might we not see the issue in reverse: instead of conservatism doing the infecting, might it not be a case of appropriation, of the cynical (or otherwise) use of conservative ideas to ensure election and re-election? Might we not see New Labour as simply using some conservative ideas and positions because it knows these to be popular? This might lead one to suggest that it is not really conservative, and that at any time it could revert to type and began re-nationalising. Of course, there are those on the left who hope this will happen as well as many on the right who fear it.

This may not be a question we can fully answer, either because people's motivations are always somewhat opaque, or because the tribal nature of politics will not allow those on the left to think benignly towards conservative ideas, however they are dressed up. But what is more interesting is to ask why it was that New Labour felt it had to pursue this route to power, and why it felt it could not continue as Old Labour? Moreover, why after getting elected three times, on each occasion with a comfortable majority, has it remained conservative? What has prevented New Labour from reverting back to old style socialism? Why, in the last chapter, were we talking about further support for owner occupation and developing choice, and not mass council housing building and the abolition of the Right to Buy? The Prime Minster did claim that he was elected as New Labour and would govern as New Labour, but why?

I want to try to deal with these questions by looking at what New Labour is, what it seems to aspire to and how it operates. We have considered what its housing policies are, and concluded they are broadly consistent with the conservative disposition. What I want to do now is to understand why a party of the centre-left that has been so successful electorally has chosen this route. It is not my intention to undertake a full discussion of such ideas as the Third Way and communitarianism and what they all mean. There is already a considerable literature on this, and I do not have the space to do justice to it[1]. But more importantly, I do not wish to dwell much on either communitarianism or the Third Way because these terms have long been jettisoned by New Labour. It no longer refers to itself as the Third Way and any sense of being part of a reinvigorated worldwide

---

[1] However, see Brown (1999) for an excellent and comprehensive discussion on housing and the Third Way, which deals well and critically with all the issues.

social democrat movement has long since fallen away since the retirement of President Clinton and the shift to the right in France, Germany and Italy. What I wish to concentrate on is what substance there is to New Labour that might differentiate it from its Conservative predecessors, and thus whether we can suggest deeper reasons for the conservative consensus in housing.

What is New Labour?

The Blair government when it came into office was portrayed (Brown, 1999, Giddens, 1994) and portrayed itself (Blair 1998) as demonstrative of a distinctly new form of politics. It sought to distinguish itself from past Labour governments and from the Conservatives that immediately preceded it. What it claimed to be doing was offering a new politics that went beyond the old verities of left and right to create a Third Way. It wished, we were told, to use those elements from each end of the spectrum that 'work', but to reject any dogmatism and preconceived notions about politics. So, for instance, Blair (1998) argued that it is not only possible, but necessary, that both social justice and wealth creation are actively encouraged by government. He suggested that:

> The Third Way stands for a modernised social democracy, passionate in its commitment to social justice and the goals of the centre-left, but flexible, innovative and forward-looking in the means to achieve them. (Blair, 1998, p. 1)

What is important in Blair's vision is that he saw no necessary contradiction in placing social justice and enterprise together. Accordingly, he states:

> My vision for the 21st century is of a popular politics reconciling themes which in the past have wrongly been regarded as antagonistic — patriotism *and* internationalism; rights *and* responsibilities; the promotion of enterprise *and* the attack on poverty and discrimination. (1998, p. 1, original emphasis)

He goes on:

> Liberals have asserted the primacy of individual liberty in a market economy; social democrats promoted social justice with the state as its main agent. There is no necessary conflict between the two, accepting as we now do that state power is one means to achieve our goals, but not the only one and emphatically not an end in itself. (p. 1)

As Brown (1999) stated, New Labour liked to talk about doing things 'that work' rather than being bound by dogma. Its flexibility, however, was such that by the time of the publication of the housing green paper in 2000 it had ceased to refer to the Third Way at all. Since then its preferred label has been 'New Labour', with little discussion on creating a new ideology.

A term it has used more consistently, and what might be seen as its defining characteristic, is its insistence on 'modernisation'. In opposition, New Labour stated that the problem with Britain was that many of its institutions were outdated and incapable of responding to the needs of a modern globalised world. The issue for the public sector, it claimed, was to reform structures and not necessarily to increase spending. As regards the constitution, it argued for devolution for Wales and Scotland and reform of the House of Lords. Since 1997 New Labour has persisted with this notion of 'modernisation', seeing it as imperative for the public sector. Even as its emphasis changed in its second and third terms, with the spending increases in health and education, it still stated an intention to reform the public sector.

However, we can question just how new and distinctive this process of modernisation actually is. Interestingly, Boyne *at al* (2003) link modernisation of the public services to public choice theory, which, as we have seen, had some influence on the Conservative governments of the 1980s and 1990s. Boyne *at al* (2003) suggest that many of the concerns raised by public choice theorists over the inefficiency and unresponsiveness of public bodies are carried over into the current government's ambitions to modernise. Therefore the current policy agenda is not particularly a break with the past, but a continuation of the policies of the 1980s and 1990s with the desire to improve efficiency by the use of market disciplines and incentives, using alternative means of provision including the private sector, and the introduction of consumer choice (Brown and King, 2005). In this sense modernisation is not particularly distinctive to New Labour at all.

But New Labour has changed from Labour governments in the past and it is necessary to recount what these changes are. Most obviously, it has abolished its long term aim of nationalising the commanding heights of the economy. This Blair considered to be a prerequisite for appearing electable and so it became a key tipping point for New Labour. Going along with the abolition of Clause Four was the general acceptance of Thatcherite settlement including privatisation and trade union reform, as well as the Conservative spending patterns for virtually the entire first term. Third, New Labour flatly refused to use the word 'socialism'. Žižek (2000) recounts an anecdote about one of the so-called 'Third Way summits' in the late 1990s. Apparently when the former Italian Prime Minister, d'Alema, said that they should not be afraid of the word 'socialism', Clinton, Blair and Schröder could not restrain themselves from bursting out laughing. Calling oneself a socialist would be seen as dreadfully unmodern, but, of course, it was also thought to be electoral suicide. Of course, this refusal to call oneself a socialist does not mean that one is necessarily a conservative. It does, however, signal a change from the past, and the refusal to be so labelled was deliberate and purposive.

However, what is interesting to question at this point is whether Blair could be considered a neoconservative? Since the withering away of the 'Third Way International' Blair has become very closely associated with President Bush and offered fulsome support for the invasions of Afghanistan and Iraq and 'the war on terror' generally. As Stelzer (2004) argues, Blair is highly regarded by neoconservatives and his views show some similarity with theirs. Indeed one of Blair's speeches is included in Stelzer's collection. The piece certainly fits comfortably with the general thrust of neoconservatism with its emphasis on activism in public policy based on a clear moral stance, and a foreign policy based on the values of democracy and freedom. We should remember that many American neoconservatives began on the left and supported President Roosevelt's New Deal in the 1930s. Indeed President Bush states that his main inspiration for his political vision comes not just from President Reagan but also from Roosevelt. This is an interesting point, which becomes more so the further the association between Blair and Bush develops.

The fourth change we can point to is a change in language away from the corporatist discourse of Old Labour and in favour of choice and opportunity. So not only does New Labour reject the label of socialism, but it also declines to 'talk' socialist. As we see below, the language used by New Labour is both different from that of its predecessors, on the right as well as the left, and is also particularly important in understanding the substance of New Labour. The fifth change is that Blair is a different form of leader from those of the past. He has no strong cultural links with the labour or trade union movements, and would not appear out of place in the Conservative party. He has thus been able to appeal to voters who would not see themselves as natural Labour supporters or who have any ideological affinity with the left.

The last change, which may appear flippant, but is indeed the most important, is that New Labour has been successful. Unlike previous Labour governments, it has not lost office in the midst of a crisis and has been able to govern for two full terms. The significance of this is that it has found a formula or set of circumstances that works for it. The other changes we have mentioned partly account for this, but we need to remember that it has not just changed from but *to* something. In the rest of this chapter I want to look at the issue of what substance there is to New Labour, and I intend to do it by considering the way in which it talks.

New Labour's Use of Words

There is a complaint that one hears frequently in the media and from its opponents, that New Labour is more concerned with presentation than with substance, that it is more concerned with newness, celebrity and difference as a political project than with the hard graft of political change. The main manner in which it creates this sense of newness is through the use of language. Its constant use of new terminology creates a sense of activity and of change, which perhaps is not matched by any actual initiatives. We have already seen that New Labour no longer refers to either communitarianism or the Third Way, the only term they have consistently used throughout their period in office being 'modernisation'. Yet it is still not clear what this means, either in terms of the 'modernised social democracy' that Blair referred to in the quotes above, or to what a modernised National Health Service would look like. When Brown (1999) attempted to define the Third Way he found it difficult and went so far as to suggest that it might be 'as much a slogan of intention as a political ideology' (p. 16). Likewise, Brown quotes Giddens, the house thinker of the Third Way, as suggesting that the term might be inappropriate because it lacks clarity. If the key thinker of the Third Way considers it unclear then we can perhaps appreciate why the term was dropped. However, this was by no means the only example of New Labour's imaginative use of language. In Brown's discussion of New Labour he shows how it continually attempts to define itself using vague and abstract phrases: it is against the class politics of left and right but is the 'modernising movement of the centre'; it eschews market fundamentalism and Keynesian demand management and is in favour of the 'new mixed economy'; it opposes both the minimal state and state corporatism with the 'new democratic state'; it rejects both the strong welfare state of Old Labour and the safety net approach of the right and puts forward the 'social investment state' (Brown, 1999, p. 17). The problem with this list of things it stands for and against is that the reader is not clear on what is meant by these terms. They sound different and new, and they seem to represent a break with the past, but just what does 'new mixed economy' and 'new democratic state' actually mean, other than the fact that they are not old?

A key element in this creation of new terms was the juxtaposition of apparent opposites so as to suggest a new synthesis. Hence we have seen that Blair wished to combine patriotism and internationalism, and enterprise and welfare. The newness of New Labour is that it aims to give us the good bits of both Old Labour and Conservatism. But the problem is that, to accommodate this juggling of two disparate ideological arguments, it has to resort to vague abstractions such as 'social investment state' and the copious use of the word 'new' as a signal for its difference. However, one might say that what New Labour represented, in its early stages at least when it was full of these juxtapositions, was government by oxymoron. The problem is that after nearly a decade in government we are no clearer on what all this means, and so we might reasonably conclude that it is not intended to mean anything new and different at all, but is rather a screen for a timid pragmatism. Instead of actually tackling the problems it identifies, it tends to redescribe them and then create an apparently new agenda that it can control. Of course, this means that it is constantly moving forwards and hence it discards the old labels including 'Third Way' and adopts new terms such as 'respect' which it hopes will embody its newly reinvented vision.

What is in question is just how much exists underneath the rhetoric and the use of fashionable concepts and ideas. We might see this practice as a rather different version of the conservative sense of governing for its own sake, of the pragmatism with a purpose that we identified with the Conservative governments in the 1980s. But because it is, as it were, playing from the other side—New Labour are a centre/left party—it must keep the left on its side and this is helped by the use of fashionable concepts. New Labour has governed largely from the right, especially if one looks at its rhetoric and policies on law and order, immigration and asylum, and welfare. Yet it has by and large managed to maintain sufficient levels of support from its traditional constituencies because of increased spending in the public sector and through a number of high-profile tokens such as banning fox-hunting which appeals to the tribal instincts of the labour movement, but which does not affect the basic balance of the economy or the state. Of course, these tokens have the effect of creating huge controversy and antipathy from the Conservative party and the right generally, but this merely assists New Labour both in maintaining its support and in perpetuating the tribal distinctions it needs to survive as a separate entity. But this practice does mean that New Labour can appear confusing (and perhaps confused). It comprises a mix of metropolitan left and liberal ideals — what the right calls 'political correctness' — with conservative and socially authoritarian politics. It can therefore ban fox-hunting and propose a ban on smoking in public places yet support a neoconservative Republican president in a series of foreign wars; it can liberalise the alcohol licensing laws yet propose laws to lock up terrorist suspects for ninety days without charge. The problem with this, of course, especially after so long in office, is that the playing off of both sides against one another can be seen as a negative, in that, instead of looking at the policies and rhetoric aimed to please us, we look at that which is meant to please our opponents. So instead of looking at immigration policy, traditional conservatives focus on the ban on fox-hunting; instead of the left seeing the extra public spending on health and education, they concentrate on the war in Iraq. So whilst both sides have something they can support, they also have an increasing amount to criticise. What this means for New Labour is that it has to increase speed and move ever more quickly in the hope of managing the increasing scepticism towards it.

We can see this constant creation of 'newness' in housing policy. Since 1997 a whole new jargon has been created, which has seen the appropriation of such terms as 'home', 'decent', 'together', 'community' and 'supporting people' to create a particular image or identity for social housing. We have seen the use of certain rather abstract words and phrases, which often do not have a precise meaning, but which are seen as 'virtuous concepts'. These have been turned into technical terms with a specific meaning somewhat at odds with their traditional definition. We can think of words such as 'home' instead of 'house' or 'dwelling unit', 'decent' instead of 'habitable' or 'good quality', and the phrase 'sustainable communities' as the specific aim of policy.

Some might argue that this is merely a semantic argument, and that what matters is not what policies are called but whether they succeed. In answer to this, how can we measure something we cannot define? More fundamentally, however, there is a suspicion that the renaming of policies and practices is essentially a displacement activity aimed at giving the impression of newness and fresh thinking, when in fact, as we have seen in chapter five, current policy is actually more a continuation of policies developed in the 1980s and 1990s. The government wants us to believe that things have changed because they have been renamed, but as we have seen, a 'step change' really means returning to the spending levels at the time when Major was Prime Minister in 1992.

We can get a sense of this tactic by looking at the very idea of a 'sustainable community'. It appears initially to show some ambition—the creation of new and vibrant communities which have all the necessary linkages and facilities—but in fact shows a rather vague sense of what its achievement might actually mean. At the root of the problem is an inability to actually define what a 'sustainable community' is. In the government's key policy document (ODPM 2003) there is no precise definition of the term, merely a series of twelve bullet points outlining the 'requirements' for a sustainable community. These points purport to tell us what makes a community sustainable, but they do not tell us what a community might be, or what it is to be sustainable. It seems to be assumed that we all already know what a community is, and the document uses the term in a common-sense manner as if there is no controversy about its usage. Instead the twelve bullet points are full of abstractions such as 'flourishing', 'strong', 'effective', 'sufficient', 'good', and so on. All of these terms are unquantifiable and question-begging, in that we are not told what it means to flourish, or how we might measure this, nor what 'effective', 'sufficient' or 'good' might actually mean. These abstract terms are all eminently laudable and describe what we would hope to achieve, but they are also vague and do not relate to anything definitive, or to any situation where we can categorically state success or failure.

In trying to come to a practical definition of a 'sustainable community' we must conclude that it boils down to *that which is deserving of government subsidy*. The term merely describes a targeted subsidy mechanism aimed at altering certain supply conditions in areas of high and low demand, creating growth and regeneration areas to meet demographic assumptions determined centrally. The term now merely has a technical meaning for a specific government policy so that neither 'sustainable' nor 'community' could now be used in any different context.

This is by no means the sole example of taking ordinary words and phrases and turning them into technical terms with a specific meaning. Government appears to consider that giving its policies and institutions what might be called soft and inclusive terms somehow alters the tenor of the policy. Amongst the policies introduced by the Blair government, we can point to the mechanism funding provision for the elderly and those with special needs banally called *Supporting People*; the policy aimed at improving housing standards in the social sector which we have discussed already in the last chapter, namely the *Decent Homes Standard* (with the consequence that a house now becomes 'decent' only if it fulfils national criteria relating to such things as the age of kitchen units and boiler, and thermal insulation); and, third, the campaign against antisocial behaviour organised by the Home Office called *Together We Can*. All these policies expropriate general expressions which can now only be used in a specific sense that empties them of any other meaning. It is now the case that a house is 'decent' because of a national standard, regardless of the views of the landlord or the person living in it. When in the autumn of 2005 the government admitted that it might not achieve full compliance with the standard by 2010, one critic asked excitedly, and apparently seriously, how tenants would feel knowing that their dwelling was not decent. More generally, a term that has connotations of politeness, respectability, conventionality, is now reduced merely to a technical term for a minimum standard. One can see the need for quality housing and the imposition of standards, but without this decline into banality.

I would argue that the reason for this use of banality is precisely because policy makers are aware of the disconnection between their policies and the manner in which housing is used. Notions of decency, togetherness and support have a natural resonance with the manner in which we live in dwelling environments and communities, and so it is hoped to gain by connecting functional policies to these terms. However, there is no change in the nature of policy making, in that these policies are national standards, assessed through top-down target setting and sanctions. All these policies have is a rather gentler, if less meaningful name (does *Together We Can* actually tell the uninitiated anything about what it is: together we can *what*?) but are no nearer to connecting with the manner in which we use our housing.

A term that came to prominence during the 2005 election campaign was *respect*. This lack of respect that government ministers claim to have identified manifests itself in antisocial behaviour, binge drinking and low-level criminality as well as a lack of civility and manners shown in public and to figures of authority such as the police and school teachers.

On one level we see here an example of politicians trying to use 'street language' to suggest that they are modern. This idea of young people insisting on respect, that they are not being 'dissed' or shown disrespect is apparently being appropriated as a major plank of public policy in Blair's third term. Perversely, of course, this is part of the problem, in that respect often means that one accepts someone regardless of what they do or say, or how they act. You are to respect someone simply because they are in front of you. This sort of respect is not about civility but self-assertion, so that what is often meant by 'respect' in some young people is that one shows the requisite level of fear towards them. The government has then picked up on a word that has come to be used in a particular way, and which it sees as having some credibility, even as it uses it in a rather different sense, in that the word also retains a rather more traditional resonance relating to civility and proper behaviour.

In 2005 the government established a 'Respect Unit' and tasked it with looking at issues such as antisocial behaviour, behaviour in schools, alcoholism and binge drinking. Its initial ideas, which were leaked to the press, included such measures as Housing Benefit sanctions for tenants evicted for antisocial behaviour, parenting orders that hold parents responsible for their child's actions, banning alcohol on public transport and altering the licensing laws in certain areas (*Sunday Telegraph*, 30 October, 2005, p. 4). One can doubt how many of these measures will be progressed — some such as Housing Benefit sanctions have been proposed and rejected before — and how many would be effective is also open to doubt, especially as many of the proposals are targeted on places rather than the individuals who are acting disrespectfully.

The problem is that we are never sure what the government is trying to deal with. It feels that there is some deep-seated social problem it needs to contend with, but which it cannot define. Like concepts such as 'modernisation', 'choice' and 'responsibility', the idea of respect is not qualified. Just as it is seldom stated what is to be modernised and why, or what we want to have choice for, or why we need to be more responsible, we are not told why we need to be more respectful, or indeed to whom we need to be more respectful. The government seeks to use categorical terms, concepts which have a history, a resonance and a general common-sense meaning — and presumably it alights on these words because of these qualities. However, it is not then prepared to come to categorical judgements about what it means to articulate the concepts and apply them fully, and this is because it fears being seen as old-fashioned and authoritarian. Accordingly, the following day after papers like the *Sunday Telegraph* published the Respect Unit's ideas, they were promptly disclaimed by ministers. As soon as there was some opposition to these proposals they were dropped and ministers suggested that they were never seriously being considered anyway.

Does this use of terms without seeing them through show that New Labour really does not fully understand the conservative disposition that it seeks to work within? I want to explore this by considering further this idea of the misuse of terminology, particularly the idea of respect. The problem with using the term in this way — to denote specific policies and actions by government — is that it gets turned into an agenda and so cannot be used in another manner: it becomes a technical term. It is, ironically, an example of disrespect towards a term with a particular general meaning and resonance. But the virtue for government is that it can use the term to encapsulate a popular mood and suggest that it is dealing with a series of issues: the government is aware that we need to deal with the lack of respect; it knows that the public is concerned by this and has established a 'unit' to deal with it. However, this initiative is often the sum total of the activity, as it is soon becomes difficult, if not impossible, to implement anything that can be definitively associated with the term.

The very convenience of these terms — their ubiquity, generality and association with common sense (what we might see as *dispositional*) — is also the reason why they are so hard to deal with in terms of policy. Indeed this is because they are not issues that government can really deal with, but relate to civil society and how individuals relate to each other. I show that I have respect for someone or something through my actions and behaviour, and not because I am prevented from drinking on a bus or because I have signed a contract with my daughter's school. Respect is not something that can be enforced from above in this manner.

The key problem is just who is best able to judge the correct level of respect that is due, or even whether respect is currently present or not? I may have a completely inflated sense of the importance of my arguments here and thus feel critics are being disrespectful if they do not concur with them or choose to ignore them. Could the government intervene here, having sensed through some mechanism or standard that my labours have not been accorded sufficient respect, and do something to compensate me or punish the disrespectful critics? Is there a justified or 'correct' level of respect that should be accorded to each individual? Is this amount equal in all cases, or would it actually be disrespectful to apply only the normal level to a high-achiever, such as an Olympic medallist or the conqueror of Everest? How do we accord the proper level of respect due to a Nobel Prize winner in chemistry compared with the winner of an Oscar; how much respect should we show the monarch compared to the prime minister? And how much of this is moderated by my own views: if I felt I should have got the Nobel prize instead of that duffer from Harvard, or if I am a republican, should I really have to be so deferential to the Queen—why cannot my views and feelings be shown equal respect—and why should I show respect to a Labour prime minister I have voted against and would like to see the back of? Of course, respect is due for different reasons—because of the position of the person or the job they do, because they are celebrated, famous, talented, charismatic and so on. But there is no definitive answer to this, and trying to find one is the trap that government has fallen into.

Instead what we do is to show common sense and display the degree of respect required according to our judgement or to some formal standard of etiquette or good manners, both of which are established by reiteration, by how we normally act. This returns us again to Oakeshott (1962) and his idea that there are certain ways of behaving and tasks we master not by instruction but from practice. We can read a book on how to drive a car but once we have finished reading it we cannot actually claim that we can drive. Rather the skill has to be practised and thus depends on reiterated actions. Likewise, our social behaviour depends on reiteration, on the repetition of actions in similar situations which are reciprocated by others. So we know how to treat a celebrated scientist and what respect is due to the prime minister regardless of his or her party allegiance (this is more pronounced in the USA where retired presidents retain their title and the deference that goes with it). These forms of behaviour become ingrained or embedded, so that we respond automatically and do so as long as the behaviour is reinforced by reciprocity and its continued general application.

What I would suggest is that the government chooses to use this term not because there is any great lack of respect, or because it is in decline, but instead because there is such a lot of it around. A government, particularly one as keen on presentation and appearance as the Blair government, would only use a term if it still had a considerable resonance. It is therefore using the term 'respect' because this is something that we see as being very important, whether it is on the street, at work, or at the dinner table. So what we can see happening here is a case of a government responding to its own perceived failure by creating a new agenda, a new sense of purpose. The first prerequisite for this new agenda is to describe it with the correct term, one which resonates properly and gives an impression of meaningful action: to say that the government is trying to inculcate respect is therefore to suggest something far-reaching and even fundamental, because respect is something very much embedded in our everyday relations. So it is precisely because there is so much respect about that government can call on the term to suggest that it is doing something important.

What we might suggest here is that New Labour consciously and deliberately goes along with a conservative agenda, using concepts like respect, yet it does so without any real desire to follow through on the logic of these concepts, perhaps out of fear of being seen as authoritarian, anti-modern or too interventionist. The result is charges of duplicity by those disappointed that the policies are not being implemented, and distrust by those who were against them in the first place and wonder why the government ever raised them as possibilities. The government is portrayed either as being weak and unprincipled by the right, or deceitful and unprincipled by the left. The problem, it seems to me, is that this tactic of triangulation, where one seeks to position oneself between two opposing sides and appeal to both, works much better for a party seeking to win an election than for a government seeking to implement a programme of policies. This is because the practice concerns itself largely with presentation and not with substantive action: it is about being seen in a particular light, but not being caught actually doing anything.

What this shows is that, whilst we can see the conservative disposition in much of what New Labour does, we should not necessarily see it in the same light as the Conservatives. The use of language to disguise a lack of action shows an opportunism, which might, of course, be seen as quintessentially Conservative—'the appetite for power' to quote Ramsden (1998)—but which perhaps also indicates a preparedness to use the conservative disposition for more cynical ends. The problem is that New Labour is a hybrid of different ideas and ideals, but as a result it has no roots in the traditions of either the left or the right, and consequently it cannot appeal to either side without creating suspicion on both sides. Neither side is prepared to accept the genuineness of New Labour and its exhortations when each has so recently seen it seeking to appease the other side.

The question that all this discussion turns on, therefore, is how genuine New Labour is in its apparent conservatism. My view is that it consists of very skilled and successful politicians who have appreciated what is needed to get elected and then stay elected. It has accepted many of the Thatcher reforms to the economy and has appropriated and then extended much of the rhetoric. In housing policy at least, this has been matched by a continuation and extension of policy.

But the issue for New Labour, and what keeps it using the prefix 'New', is that having got elected using the Conservative inheritance it cannot renege upon it and get re-elected. Having begun on this path it must follow through with it. What we might argue is that Conservatives between 1979 and 1997 so institutionalised the conservative disposition, with their rhetoric of choice and independence, but also through policies that supported owner occupation, that their successors simply have no option but to press on in this direction. Any other possibility is just not tenable, and this includes the more right-wing alternative of making loud noises about Europe or asylum. The conservative consensus is settled around a number of fixed points and this creates its own stability. The electorate, judging by the increasing numbers who see no need to vote[2], are happy with this stability and would punish any government or opposition party that sought to change it.

In the medium term—and at the time of writing New Labour's span in office is less than half of the Conservative's eighteen years—there is little alternative but to maintain the conservative consensus. One might suggest that New Labour is chipping away at it, but there is little evidence of this in housing policy or indeed in other areas of public policy where the same priorities of centralisation and choice are equally present (Brown and King, 2005). My view

---

[2] I consider the issue of apparent voter apathy and what it means in the conclusion.

is that if New Labour does continue long into the future it is not the conservative consensus that will alter, but merely what we choose to call it: New Labour, after all, is very good at finding new names for old things.

Conclusion

Keeping Things Close

I want to conclude by returning to my starting point about the significance of housing and how we relate to it. Perhaps the most important point I have sought to make, and one I have discussed at length elsewhere (King, 2004, 2005) is that housing is essentially a private activity, and it is the realisation of this by politicians since the 1980s that has driven housing policy. Such a position may appear uncongenial to many commentators on housing and to those whose careers depend on housing as a public policy issue, but it is nevertheless crucial that we understand its real significance. Hence in these final few pages I wish to draw out some of the significance of this essentially conservative insight.

Towards the end of President Clinton's second term of office in 2000 an American polling organisation, in a survey seeking to encapsulate the state of America at that point, asked the questions, 'Do you feel better off than you did 8 years ago?' and 'If so, who do you think is responsible for this?'. The latter question came with a range of possible answers including 'President Clinton', 'Congress', and 'myself'. A clear majority of respondents said 'yes' to the first question; they did indeed feel better off in 2000 compared to 1992. However, in response to the second question most felt that this was due not to the President, or to politicians at all, but was due to 'myself'. What caused comment and controversy was this second answer, where instead of being grateful to their President, the American public actually thought their increased affluence was due to their own hard work and effort. But what was really noteworthy was not the answer but the reaction to it: political commentators were actually surprised and then shocked that ordinary people looked to their own efforts and not to those of a distant politician in Washington. The consternation came with a realisation that individual Americans did not hang on every word of politicians or indeed see the world in anything like the same manner as politicians and commentators on politics.

There is a belief, which is perhaps important for politicians and those interested in politics to hold, that a community is actually defined and determined by politics. Hence we hear senior British politicians claiming that they are responsible for all manner of things such as security, public health, the cleanliness of hospitals and even global warming. We have ministers with apparent responsibility for the environment, and since 2005 we even have a cabinet minister who purports to be responsible for communities. However, what this poll in America showed was that most people do not look to politicians for a lead, but rather look to themselves. And so when barely half of the American electorate turned out to vote for either Bush or Gore later in 2000, this was not due only to apathy or to a lack of interest in the real world. It was rather because many Americans recognised that the real world was somewhere else, and somewhere closer to home, than Washington. Likewise, the considerable drop in participation in UK elections since 1992 might not be due to apathy so much as the recognition that voting just does not matter, and this is not a result of bitterness, but is caused by a general contentment. What does matter is what is around us and the one who can sort this out is 'myself'. In other words, we are largely happy with things as they are and do not much desire to change. If we feel the need to change it is likely that we will seek to do something about it ourselves, such as move house, change partner, get another job, or start to study. If we feel strongly about something such as global warming or council tax increases, we are much more likely to take part in a specific campaign than join a political party. Once this campaign is over, we will then withdraw until something else agitates us sufficiently. But, of course, most of us are never sufficiently roused in the first place, reserving ourselves to a short private grumble that all politicians are the same and so why bother to press for change. Instead we just get on with our own lives as we think best, putting those who are closest to us first.

We have, for the most part, a certain disposition that leads us towards a quiet and conditional sociability. We want to be able to engage with others and to benefit from relations with others. Yet we want to do be able to do so without being engulfed by others. We need to feel that we can withdraw when we want to and therefore maintain some control over how we live. This is what I take the old-fashioned term 'quiet enjoyment' to mean, that we can relate to others, but in a manner that is not disruptive and does not subvert our usual way of doing things. We appreciate our families and our friends, we may like to travel and see and do new things, but we want to do this in established patterns and within a framework we find normal and understandable (King, 2005). We look forward to a new book or piece of music, but do so by hunkering down into a favourite armchair in comfortable surroundings. This all sounds banal, but this is exactly what our lives are and we would not seek to change them for anything more challenging or unnerving. Much of what we do is concerned with avoiding risk and not seeing it as a challenge to be accepted with an eager relish.

The concepts I have discussed in this book, such as 'choice', 'respect' and 'responsibility', are ones to which we can and do respond positively to. We want to have a choice over what we wear and eat, where we live and who with. We know that these choices are not limitless, but neither are they negligible. We feel responsible as parents, partners, sons and daughters and also, for the majority of us, as property owners. We know what being in this relation to property brings, and we know that these very relations help us to become parents, to have stable partnerships, to help each other; having these things helps us look outwards and to be responsible, and to care. And we feel that being in this relation, and having what comes out of it, should bring with it some respect, some sense that we are contributing to maintain a stable and sustaining state of affairs. However, at the same time we want our privacy and our choices to be respected by others so that we can live in some degree of freedom.

This affects the manner in which we view government. We feel that government need not do much for us other than protect us and then leave us alone. Indeed, in this case, to protect is the same as ensuring that we are allowed to be left alone. This may indeed be quite an involved and complex set of activities, yet it is still limited in our minds to a definite role and no more.

We register the manner in which government uses certain words such as 'respect' and 'choice' which tend to resonate because we appreciate the sentiments behind them, even as we might be sceptical of the government's motives and what may result from the discourse. But still these concepts are part of what we want and see as important in our lives. We accept the terms and so it is not the case that government 'creates' them – it does not make choices or give us respect—but rather that government is responding to an accurate sense of their importance to us. This is why New Labour can get away without really doing much to operationalise these concepts and has largely done so. It is referring to what, by and large, we feel we have as a result of our own actions: it is promising to protect what we have, not to offer us something new. So not changing much need not be viewed as a negative, especially when many of us do not see the need for change and therefore see a positive virtue in keeping things as they are.

Perhaps this is the essential point about New Labour's political success. New Labour terminology involves the appropriation of the private and personal into the public. Many of the key terms are private activities or things that have a personal meaning, and hence the resonance of terms such as decent, home, choice, responsibility, respect, and so on. These concepts give policies both a veneer of sophistication aimed at taking them beyond the quotidian specificity of policy—they are dealing with 'homes' not brick boxes filled with lots of pipes, cables and wires—and a connection with deeply-held dispositions. Policy is therefore made to connect with these eminently desirable attitudes that form the general disposition of our daily lives, and so appears to be about something greater than just making sure that the pipes, cables and wires do what they are meant to do. Our house is therefore not an efficient machine but 'a decent home'. This creates the impression of going beyond the everyday and into something deeper and personal to each of us, to our sense of self, our view of ourselves as autonomous subjects—who want and need respect, responsibility and choices. In other words, New Labour has been good at articulating the language of the conservative disposition.

The beauty of this for New Labour is that, more often that not, the mere articulation of these concepts is sufficient. This is because we do not hold government responsible for the creation of our sense of respect, our freedoms and our burdens. We do not believe that these are gifts from government, but rather are things that come out of us and which are an expression of our own selves. Government can help, and this may be by massaging our sense of self with the right rhetoric, but mainly it can help through keeping out of what is closest to us.

Of course, this does not mean that things never change, or that we cease to see the need to adapt. We make changes all the time, and this is an ordinary part of social relations. But these are mostly changes at the margins. Over time it may be that these changes are so cumulatively substantial that we are no longer where we once were. But because any one change is small and the whole process is piecemeal and gradual, we perhaps do not recognise the change as out of the ordinary and disruptive. What makes this incremental change acceptable is precisely because it does not impinge on our ability to choose, our sense of responsibility, or the respect we feel we are due.

The realisation of this situation has a profound consequence for housing. The way in which we can say that the absorption of the conservative disposition into policy has apparently worked most is in *depoliticising* housing, in allowing us, as owner occupiers, to switch off from the political process itself. Owner occupation is now so dominant that it cannot become a political tool to be used for other aims and purposes, as was the case for the last time in the early 1990s when Major's government used interest rates to raise housing costs and therefore deal with inflation. What is particularly important is that our politicians now apparently know too and have circumscribed their role to that of maintaining stability. It is surely now the case in Britain that no party that does not prioritise owner occupation could be elected, and no government that has not helped owner occupation to prosper can expect re-election, as the Major government found out in 1997. It is simply unthinkable for any party to propose a housing policy that does not have the stability and prosperity of owner occupation as its centrepiece. This being the case there is no longer any battle over owner occupation and it becomes a permanent part of the political settlement that politicians can, and indeed must, take as given.

This, of course, still leaves plenty of debate over social housing, and government will doubtless continue to concern itself with this sector. However, this will remain, as it has been for over thirty years, a political backwater, where lots of earnest and necessary endeavour goes on without any great political or electoral consequence. But even here, we should remember New Labour's statement that 'Most people are well housed' (DETR/DSS, 2000, pp. 7, 15, 20) applies just as readily to social housing. Most social housing tenants live in the same manner as any owner occupier. They have rights over the property they live in which on a day-to-day basis are little different from those of an owner, and they live accordingly. They want their landlord to leave them alone and to fulfil his or her obligations as and when necessary. In return, most tenants will realise that they have a responsibility to pay their rent and maintain their tenancy regulations.

Yet governments of whatever political colour will continue to develop social housing policies and seek to deal with those who are poorly housed or without shelter at all. This will be a source of controversy and debate for those involved and interested, and the consequences will be of importance to them. But, as in the past, these debates will not transcend the popular view of housing or even be felt much beyond the boundaries of social housing itself. Social housing, we have to admit, is an area in decline; it is something of a throwback to an earlier political era before the majority had lost their illusions about what government could achieve, and consequently we expected more of government than we do now.

In any case, there is now a fully-formed political consensus on how the decline of social housing should be managed. There is no dispute on the direction that it is to take, and it is impossible to see any set of circumstances that would alter this direction. One cannot imagine what issue could so alter the existing structures, the prevailing culture and our expectations so violently that we would ever see renting from the state as ever more than a safety net for those unable to find housing for themselves. This safety net may be needed permanently and we can debate the size of it, but it is hard to take seriously any suggestion that it is more than that.

Whilst this argument may offer little comfort to those who work in and support social housing, it is also the case that this conservative consensus, at least in the sense of our relations with property, will be of little or no help to the Conservative party. Largely because of the success it had in promoting owner occupation in the 1980s and 1990s, this has largely been neutralised as a political issue, so that the Conservatives are unable to benefit other than by following a largely similar line of policy and rhetoric to that of New Labour. It is indeed unlikely that we will ever again see anything that can play so strongly for the Conservatives as the Right to Buy. Perhaps only a catastrophic collapse of the housing market will ever make it a significant political issue again, and it would be perverse in the extreme for 'the party of property ownership' to wish for this.

Of course, the problems facing the Conservative party are much wider than housing policy. However, the key point here is that there appears to be little that it can do so long as New Labour maintains its current line. As we have seen, there has been a considerable degree of continuity in housing policy over the last twenty five years. But it is also clear that if the Conservatives had won the 2005 election they would not have shifted the direction of housing policy in any substantial manner. There is little sense that the Tories have anything new to say on housing, beyond supporting owner occupation, continuing with a policy of stock transfer and maintaining a tight control of social housing activity.

What might be the biggest threat to the conservative consensus is the sheer longevity of New Labour, once it has been in office for so long that it has been able to alter the crucial institutions and change the culture in which politics operates. We shall clearly have to wait and see on this matter, but it is hard to envisage any change in the conservative consensus. After nearly a decade in power it is still unclear what New Labour stands for, and what it intends to modernise and when. Perhaps we can safely state that after three general election victories, all with sizeable majorities, it never had any real intention of radical reform and will not undertake it now. In relation to housing, as we have seen, it has tinkered at the margins and returned spending to what it was in 1992, but has also carried forward much of the Conservative agenda initiated by Thatcher in the late 1980s. What I would suggest, therefore, is that the longevity of New Labour would merely strengthen the conservative consensus. The privatisation of housing, and the manner in which it is embedded in our ordinary practices, means that housing policy itself has ceased to be relevant politically. And so long as New Labour just talk about doing things and depend on rhetoric, we should not be too concerned about the health of the conservative disposition. This does not mean we cannot be critical of New Labour. There is a vacuity at its heart and one cannot help feeling that what drives its politics is cynicism as much as principle. Yet we have to admit that much of its rhetoric is harmless to the key institutions we depend upon and that some, such as property ownership, may have actually been strengthened by this language. Those who find the conservative disposition worth protecting should therefore be grateful for New Labour's cynicism, if it has led to the more general recognition of the strength of that disposition which protects private property, supports individual choice and shows scepticism for government action.

What I have sought to show here is that this conservative disposition, and hence the consensus that it depends upon, does not rely on politics or policy. Rather, to a considerable extent, the reverse is now the case. Housing policy and the politics of housing are now so much in line with the conservative disposition that any change in direction or shift from this pattern is inconceivable. What government might feel, and we can perhaps see this in New Labour's *Homes for All* strategy (ODPM, 2005), is that it can go further in promoting owner occupation at the margins and that the promotion of choice might be extended. However, what might also be the case, and I would speculate that this will become apparent over the next decade or so, is a dying out of housing policy as a result of the combined strength of owner occupation, the increased use of personal subsidies and the continued emphasis on choice. Much more important will be the role of economic and monetary policy, including Britain's relationship with Europe, policies towards income maintenance and means testing, and the role of private providers and how they are regulated by government. This will be important for those involved in the changes and for those initiating them, but, for the majority of people, housing will have ceased to have matter as a collective political issue. What will matter much more is the way in which we are able to use our own dwelling and how this helps us to act and relate to others. As politics becomes more distant we instead see more clearly those things close to us and why they mean so much.

Bibliography

Adams, I. (1993): *Political Ideology Today*, Manchester, Manchester University Press.
Albon, R. and Stafford, D. (1987): *Rent Control*, London, Croom Helm.
Barry, N. (1986): *On Classical Liberalism and Libertarianism*, Basingstoke, Macmillan.
Blair, T. (1998): *The Third Way: New Politics for a New Century*, London, Fabian Society.
Boaz, D. (1997): 'Introduction', in Boaz, (Ed): *The Libertarian Reader: Classic and Contemporary Writings from Lao-Tzu to Milton Friedman*, New York, The Free Press, pp. xi–xviii.
Boddy, M. (1992): 'From Mutual Interests to Market Forces', in Grant, C. (Ed): *Built to Last? Reflections on British Housing Policy*, London, Roof, pp. 40-9.
Boyne, G. et al (2003): *Evaluating Public Management Reforms*, Buckingham, Open University Press.
Boyson, R. (1978): *Centre Forward: A Radical Conservative Programme*, London, Temple Smith.
Brown, T. (1999): 'The Third Way', in Brown (Ed): *Stakeholder Housing: A Third Way*, London, Pluto Press, pp. 8-32.
Brown, T. and King, P. (2005): 'The Power to Choose: Effective Choice and Housing Policy', *European Journal of Housing Policy*, Vol. 5, no. 1, pp. 59–75.
Buchanan, J. (1986): *Liberty, Market and State*, London, Harvester-Wheatsheaf.
Burke, E. (1999): *Reflections on the Revolution in France: Select Works of Edmund Burke*, vol. 2, Indianapolis, Liberty Fund.
Clapham, D. (2005): *The Meaning of Housing: A Pathways Approach*, Bristol, Policy Press.
Clark, A. (1999): *The Tories: Conservatives and the Nation State, 1992-97*, London, Pheonix.
Commission for Social Justice (1995): *Social Justice: Strategies for National Renewal*, London, Vantage (also known as the Borrie Commission report)
Conway, D. (1995): *Classical Liberalism: The Unvanquished Ideal*, Basingstoke, Macmillan.
Corry, D. (Ed) (2004): *'Choice Cuts': Essays on the Improvement of Local Services*, London, New Local Government Network.

Department of Environment (1987): *Housing: The Government's Proposals*, London, HMSO.
Department of Environment (1995): *Our Future Homes: Opportunity, Choice and Responsibility*, London, HMSO.
Department of Environment, Transport and the Regions/Department of Social Security (2000): *Quality and Choice: A Decent Home for All*, London, DETR/DSS.
Department of Work and Pensions (2002): *Building Choice and Responsibility: A Radical Agenda for Housing Benefit*, London, Department of Work and Pensions.
Devigne, R. (1994): *Recasting Conservatism: Oakeshott, Strauss, and the Response to Postmodernism*, New Haven, Yale University Press.
Ebenstein, A. (2001): *Friedrich Hayek: A Biography*, New York, St. Martin's Press.
Ferguson, A. (1966): *An Essay on the History of Civil Society*, Edinburgh, Edinburgh University Press.
Forrest, R. and Murie, A. (1988): *Selling the Welfare State: The Privatisation of Public Housing*, London, Routledge.
Friedman, F. and Friedman, R. (1980): *Free to Choose*, London, Secker & Warburg.
Fukuyama, F. (1992): *The End of History and the Last Man*, London, Hamish Hamilton.
Gamble, A. (1988): *The Free Economy and the Strong State: The Politics of Thatcherism*, Basingstoke, Macmillan.
Giddens, A. (1994): *Beyond Left and Right: The Future of Radical Politics*, Cambridge, Polity.
Green, D. (1987): *The New Right: The Counter-Revolution in Political, Economic and Social Thought*, London, Harvester-Wheatsheaf.
Green, E. (2002): *Ideologies of Conservatism*, Oxford, Oxford University Press.
Haworth, A. (1994): *Anti-libertarianism: Markets, Philosophy and Myth*, London, Routledge.
Hayek, F. (1960): *The Constitution of Liberty*, London, Routledge.
Hayek, F. (1978): *New Studies in Philosophy, Politics, Economics and the History of Ideas*, London, Routledge.
Hayek, F. (1982): *Law, Legislation and Liberty*, London, Routledge.
Hayek, F. (1988): *The Fatal Conceit: The Errors of Socialism*, London, Routledge.
Hegel, G. (1991): *Elements of the Philosophy of Right*, Cambridge, Cambridge University Press.
Heidegger, M. (1962): *Being and Time*, Oxford, Blackwell.
Hills, J. (1991): *Unravelling Housing Finance: Subsidies, Benefits and Taxation*, Oxford, Clarendon.
Honderich, T. (1990): *Conservatism*, London, Hamish Hamilton.
Hume, D. (1978): *A Treatise of Human Nature*, Oxford, Oxford University Press.
Jenkins, S. (1995): *Accountable to None: The Tory Nationalisation of Britain*, London, Hamish Hamilton.
Kant, I. (1997): *Groundwork of the Metaphysics of Morals*, Cambridge, Cambridge University Press.
Kekes, J. (1998): *A Case for Conservatism*, Ithaca, Cornell University Press.

King, P. (1996): *The Limits of Housing Policy: A Philosophical Investigation*, London, Middlesex University Press.
King, P. (1998): *Housing, Individuals and the State: The Morality of Government Intervention*, London, Routledge.
King, P. (2000): 'Individuals and Competence', in King and Oxley, pp. 9–69.
King, P. (2001): *Understanding Housing Finance*, London, Routledge.
King, P. (2003): *A Social Philosophy of Housing*, Aldershot, Ashgate.
King, P. (2004): *Private Dwelling: Contemplating the Use of Housing*, Abingdon, Routledge.
King, P. (2005): *The Common Place: the Ordinary Experience of Housing*, Aldershot, Ashgate.
King, P. and Oxley, M. (2000): *Housing: Who Decides?*, Basingstoke, Macmillan.
Kirk, R. (1985): *The Conservative Mind: From Burke to Eliot*, 7th revised edition, Washington, Regnery Press.
Koppl, R. (1994): 'Invisible Hand Explanations', in Boettke, P. (Ed): *The Elgar Companion to Austrian Economics*, Aldershot, Edward Elgar, pp. 192–6.
McCue, J (1997): *Edmund Burke and our Present Discontents*, London, Claridge Press.
Malpass, P. (Ed) (1986): *The Housing Crisis*, London, Croom Helm.
Malpass, P. (1990): *Reshaping Housing Policy: Subsidies, Rents and Residualisation*, London, Routledge.
Malpass, P. (2005): *Housing and the Welfare State: The Development of Housing Policy in Britain*, Basingstoke, Palgrave.
Malpass, P. and Aughton, H. (1999): *Housing Finance: A Basic Guide*, 5th edition, London, Shelter.
Malpass, P. and Murie, A. (1999): *Housing Policy and Practice*, 5th edition, Basingstoke, Macmillan.
Mandeville, B. (1988): *The Fable of the Bees: or Private Vices, Publick Benefits*, 2 vols, Indianapolis, Liberty Fund.
Marsh A., Cowan, D., Cameron, A., Jones, M., Kiddle, C. and Whitehead, C. (2004): *Piloting Choice-Based Lettings: An Evaluation*, London, ODPM.
Mises, L. (1981): *Socialism: An Economic and Sociological Analysis*, Indianapolis, Liberty Fund.
Muller, J. (1997): 'Introduction: What is Conservative Social and Political Thought?', in Muller, J. (Ed): *Conservatism: An Anthology of Social and Political Thought from David Hume to the Present*, Princeton, Princeton University Press, pp. 3–31.
Narveson, J. (1988): *The Libertarian Idea*, Philadelphia, Temple University Press.
Niskanen, W. (1973): *Bureaucracy: Servant or Master?*, London, Institute for Economic Affairs.
Nozick, R. (1974): *Anarchy, State and Utopia*, Oxford, Blackwell.
Nozick, R. (1997): *Socratic Puzzles*, Cambridge, Mass., Harvard University Press.
Oakeshott, M. (1962): *Rationalism in Politics and Other Essays*, new and expanded edition, Indianapolis, Liberty Press.
Office of the Deputy Prime Minister (2003): *Sustainable Communities: Building for the Future*, London, ODPM.

Office of the Deputy Prime Minister (2005): *Sustainable Communities: Homes for All: A Five Year Plan from the ODPM*, London, ODPM.

O'Hara, K. (2005): *After Blair: Conservatism Beyond Thatcher*, Cambridge, Icon.

Pawson, H. (2004): 'Reviewing Stock Transfer', in Wilcox, S. (Ed): *UK Housing Review, 2004/2005*, pp. 11-19.

Pleace, N., Burrows, R. and Quilgers, D. (1997): 'Homelessness in Contemporary Britain: Conceptualisation and Measurement', in Burrows, R., Pleace, N. and Quilgers, D. (Eds.): *Homelessness and Social Policy*, London, Routledge, pp. 1–18.

Power, A. (1987): *Property Before People: The Management of Twentieth Century Council Housing*, Hemel Hempstead, Allen & Unwin.

Pratchett, L. (2002): 'Local Government: From Modernisation to Consolidation', *Parliamentary Affairs*, Vol. 55, pp 331–46.

Quinton, A. (1993): 'Conservatism', in Goodin, R. and Pettit, P. (Eds.): *A Companion to Contemporary Political Philosophy*, Oxford, Blackwell, pp. 244–68.

Ramsden, J. (1998): *An Appetite for Power: A History of the Conservative Party since 1830*, London, Harper Collins.

Rasmussen, D. and Den Uyl, D. (1991): *Liberty and Nature: An Aristotelian Defence of Liberal Order*, La Salle, Open Court.

Richards, J. (1992): 'A Sense of Duty', in Grant, C (Ed): *Built to Last? Reflections on British Housing Policy*, London, Roof, pp. 129–38.

Roberts, A. (1999): *Salisbury: Victorian Titan*, London, Weidenfeld & Nicholson.

Saunders, P. (1990): *A Nation of Home Owners*, London, Allen & Unwin.

Scott, J. (1995): *Sociological Theory: Contemporary Debates*, Aldershot, Edward Elgar.

Scruton, R. (2000): *England: An Elegy*, London, Chatto & Windus.

Scruton, R (2001): *The Meaning of Conservatism*, 3rd edition, Basingstoke, Palgrave.

Seldon, A (1977): *Charge*, London, Temple Smith.

Seldon, A. (2005): *The Virtues of Capitalism: Collected Works, Vol. 1*, Indianapolis, Liberty Fund.

Shand, A. (1990): *Free Market Morality: The Political Economy of the Austrian School*, London, Routledge.

Shepherd, R. (1996): *Enoch Powell: A Biography*, London, Hutchinson.

Skidelsky, R. (1995): *The World After Communism: A Polemic for our Times*, London, Macmillan.

Smith, A. (1976a): *An Inquiry into the Nature and Causes of the Wealth of Nations*, 2 vols, Indianapolis, Liberty Fund.

Smith, A. (1976b): *The Theory of Moral Sentiments*, Indianapolis, Liberty Fund.

Stelzer, I. (Ed) (2004): *Neoconservatism*, London, Atlantic Books.

Tulloch, G. (1976): *The Vote Motive*, London, Institute of Economic Affairs.

Turner, J. F. C. (1976): *Housing by People: Towards Autonomy in Building Environments*, London, Marion Boyars.

Ward, C. (1985): *When We Build Again, Let's Have Housing That Works*, London, Pluto Press.

Wilcox, S. (Ed) (2004): *UK Housing Review, 2004/2005*, York, Joseph Rowntree Foundation/Chartered Institute of Housing/Council for Mortgage Lenders.

Wittgenstein, L. (1958): *Philosophical Investigations*, Oxford, Blackwell.

Wolff, J. (1991): *Robert Nozick: Property, Justice and the Minimal State*, Cambridge, Polity.

Žižek, S. (2000): *The Fragile Absolute: Or, Why is the Christian Legacy Worth Fighting For?*, London, Verso.

Index

Adams, I 21
Afghanistan 40n5, 60, 128
antisocial behaviour 134
Aristotle 13
arms length management organisation (ALMO) 102, 109, 110-11
Asquith, H 79
Atlee, C 9, 123
Audit Commission 10
autonomy 117

Baldwin, S 79
Balfour, A 65
Blair, T 1, 3, 12, 13, 17, 19, 37, 39n4, 45n6, 97, 99, 107n2, 126, 128, 129; government of 121-39
Boaz, D 49-50
bourgeois family 43
Boyne, G 127
Brown, G 104
Brown, T 125n1, 127, 129
Buchanan, J 59
Burke, E 27, 30, 31, 37, 56, 69
Bush G W 26, 128, 142

Camden 111
capitalism, 1-2, 60-1, 74
centralisation 89-90, 101, 103-4, 105, 111-2, 116, 121, 138-9, 147
Chamberlain, N 79
Chesterton, G K 74, 79
choice 8, 12, 48, 59, 104, 107, 116-9, 121, 125, 127, 134-5, 139, 143-4, 148
Churchill, W 9, 78
Clapham, D 103
Clark, A 65, 80
Clarke, K 95
classical liberalism 21-2, 48, 51, 55, 59, 61, 74, 80, 85
Clinton, B 128, 141
Commission for Social Justice 115

communism 66
community charge 70; see also Poll Tax
conservatism, definition of 26-46
conservative disposition 6, 18-19, 22-4, 27, 62-3, 68-70, 96, 121-6, 138-9, 144-8
Conway, D 48
council housing 8, 9, 13, 43, 78-9
cultural condition of politics 24-5, 123-4

d'Alema, M 128
Decent Homes Standard 107-8, 118, 133
decommodification 91-2
Democratic Party 23
Den Uyl, D 49
depoliticisation of housing 145
Devigne, R 61, 62
distribution 53

Ebenstein, A 25, 54
Eden, A 9, 66
equality 12, 54
Euro 17
Europe 148
evolutionary conservatism 33-4; see also Oakeshott
Exchange Rate Mechanism 95

fatalism 37
Ferguson, A 55
Forrest, R 91
Friedman, M 49, 57-9, 60, 62
Fukuyama, F 12

Gamble, A 85
Giddens, A 3, 14, 23, 26-7, 28, 73, 124, 129
Gore, A 142
Green, D 59
Green, E 65

Hayek F 25, 31-2, 34, 47, 48, 49, 54-7, 59, 60, 61-2, 74, 79, 85
Heath, E 23, 66, 74, 85, 86
Hegel, G 12, 28, 39, 40, 41, 49
Heidegger, M 34
Hills, J 13-14
home 43, 144
Homes for All 97, 100, 103, 114, 148
Honderich, T 38, 41, 44-5, 119
House of Lords 37, 122
Housing Act 1980 87
Housing Act 1988 83
Housing Action Trusts 83
Housing Benefit 80, 81-2, 83, 88-9, 98, 105, 106, 107n2, 117-8, 134
Housing Corporation 104, 111
Housing Finance Act 1972 86
Housing Green Paper 2000 6-7, 11, 15, 96-7, 100, 105, 110, 119
Housing (Homeless Persons) Act 1977, 11
Housing Market Package 95
Housing White Paper 1987 6, 15, 90-1, 115, 119
Housing White Paper 1995 15
Hume, D 55, 56

ideology 8-16, 18, 19, 21-6, 65-8, 73-6, 123-6
individualism 28-9
Iraq 17, 40n5, 60, 128
invisible hand 55

Jenkins, S 89, 105, 122
Joseph K 25

Kant, I 52
Kantian 29;
 Categorical Imperative 52
Kekes, J 29-30, 33, 36, 38
Keynesian 57, 129
Kirk, R 27

Lao-Tzu 49
large scale voluntary transfer 83;
 see also stock transfer
liberal 47-8
libertarianism 19, 25, 34, 46, 47-63, 65, 66-8, 124;
 defined 49-54
Local Government and Housing Act 1889 82, 87

Macmillan, H 9, 65, 66, 79, 81, 85, 99
Major, J 6, 62, 65, 66, 80, 89, 94, 100, 103, 119, 122, 132, 145

Malpass, P 11, 81, 93
Mandeville, B 47, 48, 55, 56
Marxism 19, 21-2, 40, 43, 44, 67
Mill, J S, 47, 48, 49, 65
Mises, L 34, 85
modernisation 10, 17, 67, 122, 127, 129, 134-5
monetarism 57
mortgage interest tax relief (MITR) 88, 94, 95, 96
Muller, J 37
Murie, A 81, 91, 93

Narveson, J 49
National Health Service 13, 61, 78-9, 129
need 12
neo-conservatism 45n6, 128
Niskanen, W 59, 60
Nozick, R 35n3, 49, 50-4, 55, 57, 66-7

Oakeshott, M 33-5, 38, 56, 61-2, 68, 74, 78, 84-5, 86, 90, 122, 136
object subsidies 87
Office of the Deputy Prime Minister (ODPM) 111
O'Hara K 23, 26
organicism 39-41
owner occupation 8, 17-18, 23, 44, 76, 85, 98, 101, 116, 119, 148;
 see also private property ownership

particularism 24
Peabody Trust 10
philosophical conservatism 3, 14, 23, 26, 73, 124
Plato 13
Pol Pot 66
Poll Tax 17; see Community Charge
Powell, E 81
pragmatism 13-15, 19, 24, 45-6, 62-3, 65-71, 74, 76-84, 96, 105, 123
Prescott, J 113
privacy 4, 44-5, 144
private finance 100, 104, 109-12, 116
Private Finance Initiative (PFI) 23, 102, 103, 109, 111
private property ownership 2, 13, 17, 38, 41-5, 46, 48, 62-3, 75, 80, 90-7, 105, 121, 146;
 entitlement to 52-3;
 see owner occupation
privatisation 70
public choice 59-60, 127

Index

Quinton A 21, 29-33, 35-6, 39-40, 44

radicalism 13-15, 26-7
Ramsden, J 63, 65, 80, 138
Rasmussen, D 49
rationality 38;
  constructivist 56;
  evolutionary 56
Raynsford, N 117
Reagan, R 3, 26, 128
rent controls 9, 79-82, 85, 90, 106
rent restructuring 106-7
rents 86, 100, 104
resource accounting 108-9, 116
respect 67, 134-7, 143-4
Respect Unit 134, 135
responsibility 8, 42, 134-5, 143-4
Right to Buy 3, 5, 6, 8, 9, 13, 15, 19, 44, 70-1, 87, 91, 92-4, 112, 114, 119, 125, 146
rights 42, 51
Roberts, A 69
Roosevelt, F 128

Salisbury, Lord 69, 80
Salisbury Review, The 60
Saunders, P 2
scepticism 33-9, 105
Schröder, G 128
Scruton, R 27-9, 30-1, 32, 34-5, 39, 41-5, 49, 60, 68, 74, 85, 115, 122
Seldon, A 47, 48, 58, 59, 60, 61, 62, 66, 76
Shepherd, R 81
shock therapy 14
side-constraint 51
Smith, A 47, 48, 55, 56
social justice 12, 56-7, 115, 126
socialism 99, 128
Spencer, H 47
spontaneity 55
Stelzer, I 128
stock transfer 7, 82-4, 90, 101, 102, 103, 109, 110, 116, 147
subject subsidies 87
Suez, 65
Supporting People 133
sustainable community, definition of 132-3
Sustainable Communities Plan 88, 100, 103, 112-4, 115-6

Tenants' Choice 83, 92-4, 112
Thatcher, M 1, 3, 5, 6, 13, 17, 26, 39n4, 46, 54, 61, 62, 65, 66, 70, 74, 76, 85, 86, 92, 99, 100, 101, 104, 122, 123, 138, 147
Thatcherism 25, 27, 84
Third Way 10, 12, 22, 67, 100, 125n1, 126, 127, 129, 130
Together We Can 133-4
traditionalism 29-32
Treasury 104, 110, 111
Tulloch, G 59
Turner, J 44

unintended consequences 30, 33, 55

vouchers 58

war on terror 60, 128
Ward, C 44
Weber M 23
Wilcox, S 101
Wittgenstein 34

Žižek, S 12, 128

British politics from imprint-academic.com

The Gypsy Debate: Can discourse control?
Jo Richardson

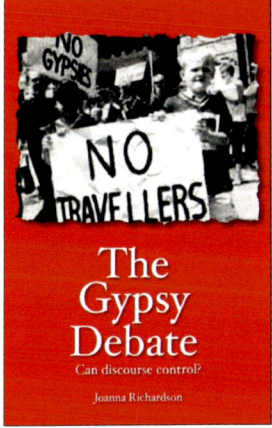

'They are scum, and do not deserve the same human rights as my decent constituents going about their everyday lives.' So declared Andrew MacKay, MP for Bracknell, speaking of gypsies and travellers in the House of Commons in 2002.

Jo Richardson explores the extent to which such discourse not only reflects antipathy towards gypsies and travellers, but also has a power to control and shape the treatment of this minority group by the rest of society. The author is senior lecturer in the Centre for Comparative Housing Research at De Montfort University, Leicester.

200 pp., £17.95 / $34.90, 1845400577 (pbk.)

A Conservative Consensus? Housing policy before 1997 and after
Peter King

New Labour would like to portray 1997 as a new beginning for public policy, but Peter King argues that we now have, in housing and in other areas of public policy, a consensus based on Thatcherite reforms. He explores the particularly conservative understanding of housing that transformed public attitudes in the 1980s and 1990s, and the impact it still has on policy. This book is written with non-housing specialists in mind. The author is Reader in Social Thought in the Centre for Comparative Housing Research at De Montfort University, Leicester.

200 pp., £17.95 / $34.90, 1845400461 (pbk.)

Principles and Politics in Contemporary Britain
Mark Garnett

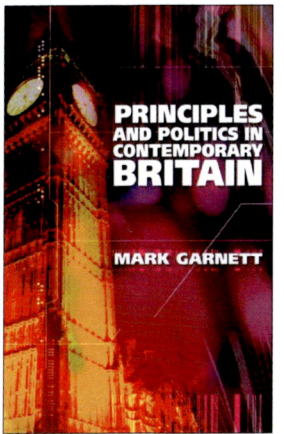

This book shows the importance of political ideas in policy-making and demonstrates the extent to which pragmatic considerations preclude the imposition of rigid ideological programmes. It charts the decline of the postwar British 'consensus', the changing face of both the Conservative and Labour parties under the long shadow of Thatcherism, and the growing emergence of single issue policies such as environmentalism and feminism.

This second edition is completely revised and updated.

'Heartily recommended ... lively and provocative.'
David Denver, *Parliamentary Affairs*

250 pp., £17.95 / $34.90, 1845400267 (pbk.)

British politics from imprint-academic.com

Paradoxes of Power: Reflections on the Thatcher interlude
Alfred Sherman, edited by Mark Garnett

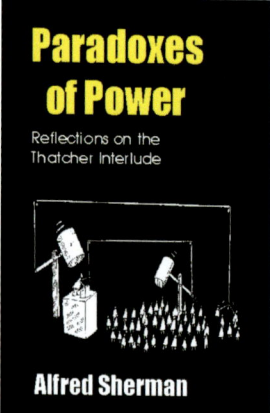

This book describes Sherman's early relationship with Sir Keith Joseph and his own role in the formation of the Centre for Policy Studies in 1974. Sherman examines the origins and development of 'Thatcherism', but concludes that the Conservative administrations of the 1980s were, primarily, an 'interlude' and that the post-war consensus remains largely unscathed — 'we are back where we started'.

'These reflections by Thatcherism's inventor are necessary reading.' **Sir John Hoskyns**, *Salisbury Review*

'This book should be read by anyone examining the 1970s Conservative renaissance.' **Margaret Thatcher**

200 pp., £17.95 / $34.90, 1845400143 (cloth)

The Rape of the Constitution?
Keith Sutherland (ed.)

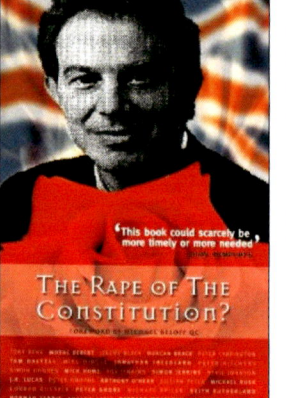

Lord Hailsham once remarked that if you removed a brick from the wall of the British constitution, the building was likely to collapse; yet New Labour has embarked on a reckless and unprecedented path of constitutional change. Has the steady increase in executive power turned Bagehot's 'disguised republic' into an elective dictatorship? This book includes chapters by scholars, politicians and journalists who have thought deeply about these issues.

'Timely and important.' *Times Literary Supplement*

'To be enjoyed by all who love freedom and democracy and mistrust the aspirations of the state.'
Chris Woodhead, *Sunday Telegraph*

384 pp., £14.95 / $25.90, 0907845703 (pbk.)

New Labour's Old Roots: Revisionist thinkers in Labour's history 1931–1997
Patrick Diamond (ed.)

New Labour was not conjured up out of thin air — it only looks like that because of the party's amnesia concerning its intellectual development. This book provides extracts from fifteen thinkers located within the revisionist tradition as an antidote to that amnesia, including Tawney, Jay, Crosland, Gaitskell and Gordon Brown. The collection shows that revisionism is not a body of doctrine but a cast of mind that distinguishes between core values (ends) and policy instruments (means). In the contentious debates about the future of public services, the Blair government is determined to avoid the confusion of means and ends.

264 pp., £17.95 / $29.90, 0907845894 (pbk.)